KETO DIET
FOR WOMEN OVER 50

The Complete 28-Day Meal Plan To Burn Fat And Lose Weight Quickly Without Giving Up On Foods You Love By Preparing Easy, Tasty, And Light Recipes

Emily Ross

© Copyright 2021 by Emily Ross - All rights reserved.

This document is geared towards providing exact and reliable information in regard to the topic and issue covered.

- From a Declaration of Principles which was accepted and approved equally by a Committee of the American Bar Association and a Committee of Publishers and Associations.

In no way is it legal to reproduce, duplicate, or transmit any part of this document in either electronic means or in printed format. All rights reserved.

The information provided herein is stated to be truthful and consistent, in that any liability, in terms of inattention or otherwise, by any usage or abuse of any policies, processes, or directions contained within is the solitary and utter responsibility of the recipient reader. Under no circumstances will any legal responsibility or blame be held against the publisher for any reparation, damages, or monetary loss due to the information herein, either directly or indirectly.

Respective authors own all copyrights not held by the publisher.

The information herein is offered for informational purposes solely and is universal as so. The presentation of the information is without contract or any type of guarantee assurance.

The trademarks that are used are without any consent, and the publication of the trademark is without permission or backing by the trademark owner. All trademarks and brands within this book are for clarifying purposes only and are owned by the owners themselves, not affiliated with this document.

Table of Contents

INTRODUCTION 8

CHAPTER 1: BASICS FOR CORRECT APPROACH TO EVERY DIET 10
- Tips to Keep Motivation High 10

CHAPTER 2: TRICKS TO KEEP MOTIVATION HIGH 14
- Prepare in Advance for How You'll Face Challenges 14
- Importance of a Good Hydration 15
- Right Amount of Calories per Day 16
- Healthy Habits 16

CHAPTER 3: TECHNICAL ASPECTS 18
- Important to Know During a Diet 18

CHAPTER 4: MACROS—WHAT ARE AND SUBDIVISION 24
- Explanation about Macros 24
- Fats 24
- Proteins 26
- Carbohydrates 27

CHAPTER 5: KETOSIS 30
- What Is It? 30
- How Does It Work? 30
- Signals to Understand We Are in Ketosis 31

CHAPTER 6: KETOGENIC DIET 32
- What Food Based On 32
- Foods to Be Consumed in Moderation 32
- Foods to Avoid 34

CHAPTER 7: MACROS INVOLVED PERCENT SUBDIVISION 36
- Advantages of the Keto Diet and Benefits 37
- Common mistake and Issues 38
- Intoxication 39

CHAPTER 8: TIPS FOR WOMEN OVER 50 42
- Tips for Women Over 60 43

CHAPTER 9: BREAKFAST RECIPES 48
1. Chocolate Protein Pancakes 48
2. Frittata 49
3. Bacon and Zucchini Muffins 50
4. Blueberry Pancake Bites 51

5.	Pretzels	52
6.	Breakfast Omelet with Mushrooms	53
7.	Morning Coconut Porridge	54
8.	Sesame Keto Bagels	55
9.	Baked Eggs in Avocado Halves	56
10.	Spicy Cream Cheese Pancakes	57
11.	Almond Flour Keto Pancakes	58
12.	Keto Coconut Flour Egg Muffin	59
13.	Broccoli Cheddar Cheese Muffins	60
14.	Chicken, Bacon, Avocado Caesar Salad	61
15.	Coconut Macadamia Bars	62
16.	Macadamia Chocolate Fat Bomb	63
17.	Keto Lemon Breakfast Fat Bombs	64
18.	Cheese Crepes	65
19.	Ricotta Pancakes	66
20.	Yogurt Waffles	67
21.	Broccoli Muffins	68
22.	Pumpkin Bread	69
23.	Eggs in Avocado Cups	70
24.	Cheddar Scramble	71
25.	Bacon Omelet	72
26.	Green Veggies Quiche	73
27.	Chicken & Asparagus Frittata	74
28.	Southwest Scrambled Egg Bites	75
29.	Bacon Egg Bites	76
30.	Omelet Bites	77
31.	Cheddar & Bacon Egg Bites	78
32.	Avocado Pico Egg Bites	79
33.	Salmon Scramble	80
34.	Mexican Scrambled Eggs	81
35.	Caprese Omelet	82
36.	Sausage Omelet	83
37.	Brown Hash with Zucchini	84
38.	Crunchy Radish & Zucchini Hash Browns	85
39.	Fennel Quiche	86
40.	Turkey Hash	87

CHAPTER 10: LUNCH RECIPES 88

41.	Meatballs	88
42.	Rainbow Mason Jar Salad	89
43.	Fish Cakes	90
44.	Lasagna Stuffed Peppers	91
45.	Korean Ground Beef Bowl	92
46.	Shrimp Lettuce Wraps with Buffalo Sauce	93
47.	Poke Bowl with Salmon and Veggies	94
48.	Thai Cucumber Noodle Salad	95
49.	Wrapped Bacon Cheeseburger	96

50.	Hearty Lunch Salad with Broccoli and Bacon	97
51.	Fatty Burger Bombs	98
52.	Avocado Taco	99
53.	Chicken Quesadillas	100
54.	Salmon Sushi Rolls	101
55.	Mediterranean Salad with Grilled Chicken	102
56.	Creamy Cauliflower Soup	103
57.	Easy Keto Smoked Salmon Lunch Bowl	104
58.	Easy One-Pan Ground Beef and Green Beans	105
59.	Easy Spinach and Bacon Salad	106
60.	Easy Keto Italian Plate	107
61.	Fresh Broccoli and Dill Keto Salad	108
62.	Keto Smoked Salmon Filled Avocados	109
63.	Low-Carb Broccoli Lemon Parmesan Soup	110
64.	Prosciutto and Mozzarella Bomb	111
65.	Summer Tuna Avocado Salad	112
66.	Mushrooms & Goat Cheese Salad	113
67.	Keto Bacon Sushi	114
68.	Cole Slaw Keto Wrap	115
69.	Keto Chicken Club Lettuce Wrap	116
70.	Keto Broccoli Salad	117
71.	Keto Sheet Pan Chicken and Rainbow Veggies	118
72.	Skinny Bang-Bang Zucchini Noodles	119
73.	Keto Caesar Salad	120
74.	Keto Buffalo Chicken Empanadas	121
75.	Pepperoni and Cheddar Stromboli	122
76.	Tuna Casserole	123
77.	Brussels Sprout and Hamburger Gratin	124
78.	Carpaccio	125
79.	Keto Croque Monsieur	126
80.	Keto Wraps with Cream Cheese and Salmon	127
81.	Savory Keto Broccoli Cheese Muffins	128

CHAPTER 11: DINNER RECIPES 130

82.	Mexican Shredded Beef	130
83.	Beef Stew	131
84.	Coconut Shrimp	132
85.	Sausage Stuffed Zucchini Boats	133
86.	Balsamic Steaks	134
87.	Chicken Pan with Veggies and Pesto	135
88.	Cabbage Soup with Beef	136
89.	Cauliflower Rice Soup with Chicken	137
90.	Quick Pumpkin Soup	138
91.	Fresh Avocado Soup	139
92.	Green Chicken Curry	140
93.	Creamy Pork Stew	141
94.	Salmon & Shrimp Stew	142

95.	Chicken Casserole	143
96.	Creamy Chicken Bake	144
97.	Beef & Veggie Casserole	145
98.	Beef with Bell Peppers	146
99.	Braised Lamb shanks	147
100.	Shrimp & Bell Pepper Stir-Fry	148
101.	Veggies & Walnut Loaf	149
102.	Keto Sloppy Joes	150
103.	Low Carb Crack Slaw Egg Roll in a Bowl Recipe	151
104.	Low Carb Beef Stir Fry	152
105.	One Pan Pesto Chicken and Veggies	153
106.	Crispy Peanut Tofu and Cauliflower Rice Stir-Fry	154
107.	Simple Keto Fried Chicken	155
108.	Keto Butter Chicken	156
109.	Keto Shrimp Scampi Recipe	157
110.	Keto Lasagna	158
111.	Creamy Tuscan Garlic Chicken	159
112.	Ancho Macho Chili	160
113.	Chicken Supreme Pizza	161
114.	Baked Jerked Chicken	162
115.	Chicken Schnitzel	163
116.	Broccoli and Chicken Casserole	164
117.	Baked Fish with Lemon Butter	165

CHAPTER 12: 28-DAY MEAL PLAN 166

Grocery List 166
Meal Plan 167

CONCLUSION 170

INTRODUCTION

The ketogenic diet is the basis for a weight-loss regimen that has become popular with health experts and nutritionists who emphasize the benefits of cutting down on carbohydrates. According to dietitians, as we grow older, we put on weight because of the less active lifestyle and dietary habits changes. It can be detrimental as it may lead to several health issues, including diabetes, cardiac problems, obesity, etc. However, the health experts think that the best way to deal with these problems is to adopt a Keto Diet and shed all the excess weight. As per experts, the reason is that it provides many health benefits, including reducing fat in the body, improving insulin levels, and regulating blood glucose levels.

One of the most common misconceptions associated with Ketogenic diets is that those who adopt them will be left hungry. It is far from the truth. What is provided in the Ketogenic diet is high-fat content, thus it helps to replenish the body's essential nutrients. The recommended fat intake is around 80 percent of total calories. It makes it possible for women to lose weight healthily and maintain their body fitness level as well. Women are often concerned about their weight and want to control it. It is important to know that women over 50 may present specific health issues because of aging and hormonal changes, and an unhealthy diet or lifestyle. Here, a Ketogenic diet might be the best way to balance these problems. This way of eating significantly reduces carbohydrates intake and increases fat intake. It means that the brain can rely on internal sources of energy instead of using glucose. It means that the body produces ketones.

Many women over 50 are experiencing digestive issues, leading to a reduced quality of life; including depression and fatigue. Many women have noticed decreasing muscle mass as they get older, which can cause pain and decreased mobility.

Women over 50 can benefit from the Ketogenic diet because it may help improve symptoms of menopause and help maintain a healthy metabolism and blood sugar levels. The Ketogenic diet may also slow down skeletal muscle breakdown as people age, which matters in maintaining strength and muscle mass.

Another benefit from the Ketogenic diet: weight loss. While weight loss is a primary goal for many women over 50, this diet can be beneficial in reducing fat from the abdominal area. It is because abdominal fat becomes more concentrated in women over 50.

Women over 50 may also experience specific health issues such as insulin resistance, prediabetic, heart disease, and polycystic ovarian syndrome (PCOS). The Ketogenic diet appears to help with these issues.

At mealtime, keep it small and include lots of healthy fats. A good rule is to make a breakfast that comprises fat and protein and avoid adding carbohydrates. For lunch and dinner, keep these simple. Many high-fat meals can be eaten at one time or split into two meals. If you do not want to incorporate more fat into your daily diet, then have a keto-friendly smoothie for breakfast. If you do not like eating red meat, then opt for a fish or chicken instead. However, if you are picking chicken or fish, make sure that it is skinless to add not too much fat and keep it within your daily fat limit.

This diet can also improve sleep quality, reduce aches and pains, help with constipation issues due to the high fiber in this diet, and reduce PMS symptoms. On the other hand, this diet can also pose some side effects, including the following: Constipation (the high fiber content in this diet is a good thing but can cause problems for some).

Keto flu is a temporary condition that affects many people who start on the Ketogenic diet. It includes feeling tired, having difficulty focusing, having bad breath, and experiencing headaches. These symptoms occur because your brain needs time to adjust to using ketones instead of glucose for fuel. These symptoms can occur in the first few days of starting this diet or may not appear until several weeks after.

The Ketogenic diet has not been studied a lot in this age group, and there is no long-term data on its effects. This diet may lead to health problems such as kidney damage or an increased risk for bone fractures. Therefore, you need to discuss this diet in more detail with your doctor.

CHAPTER 1:

BASICS FOR CORRECT APPROACH TO EVERY DIET

Tips to Keep Motivation High

Knowing what to eat is a critical piece of the weight loss puzzle, but having the mindset and motivation to stick with it over the long haul is an equally important, if not more important, piece of the puzzle. Here is a Top Ten list for ways to get your head in the game, keep yourself engaged and inspired, and see this through to your goal weight.

Define Your Why

You might have a wide variety of reasons for starting a weight loss program right now. Jot them down and reflect on them. Putting them in writing helps you keep them on top of your mind, and regularly reading through them can keep you motivated.

You might sight your appearance as a reason. Maybe you want to look more comfortable in your clothes, reach a smaller size, or have a more fit body. Perhaps your reasons center more around how you feel. Sleeping better at night, having more energy during the day, and experiencing more mental clarity can all serve as powerful motivators.

Your reasons may be more about current or at-risk health conditions like preventing or managing diabetes, reducing your risks of heart attack, cancer, or stroke. You might notice that some of your reasons connect to other people in your life. It's common for women over fifty to want to be healthy enough to keep up with their grandchildren or to feel confident when you accompany your significant other to a work event. Your doctor might have been the one to suggest a weight loss plan, so getting an excellent report at your next visit might keep you in the game.

There's not a single right or wrong reason for wanting to be the best version of yourself. Keeping the reasons why this is important to you close to your heart and reflecting on them will often help keep you focused or centered and contribute to your motivation to continue even when the newness wears off.

Keep Your Eyes on the Prize

You might have a final weight goal in mind; the desired outcome you want to accomplish at the end. Most of the time, that long-term goal is the final target weight you are working to reach. But if you only focus on the long-term outcome-based goals, you might find your motivation lacking along the way, particularly if getting to that goal will probably take you a while.

It is equally important to have and commit to writing short-term goals that are more process-based than outcome-based. A process goal is simply an action you make to take you one step closer to your desired outcome.

For example, you might choose to set a long-term goal to lose twenty-five pounds.

You might set a process goal for yourself to exercise for thirty minutes per day, four days per week.

Keeping your eyes on the prize and paying attention to your small process goals will help you achieve your desired outcome.

Be Realistic About the Pace

You might have watched television programs, read books, or heard examples of people losing weight at a shockingly quick pace. Several trendy diet programs and products tout easy and fast weight loss. But if you ask the medical community experts, they will recommend a loss of 1-2 pounds per week.

Regardless of the number of pounds you hope to lose, you will enjoy benefits to your health and well-being. Every pound makes a difference. Research shows that a 5% loss contributes benefits to your overall health. Ponder how beneficial it would be to shed 10% of your body weight. Suppose your starting weight is 190 pounds, for example, and you lose 9-19 pounds. In that case, you are statistically likely to see improved blood sugar control, reduced joint pain, reduced risks of certain types of cancer, reduced risk of heart disease, and lower cholesterol levels.

Don't set your goals out of reach, and don't expect to lose at an unnatural rate. Unattainable goals and unreasonable expectations can contribute to feelings of failure and frustration, and cause you to give up. Conversely, reaching a goal that you set, worked toward, and achieved contributes to feelings of success, empowerment, and accomplishment.

Keep a Journal

Consider keeping a journal to record milestones, track your progress, and make a note of your thoughts and feelings along the way. You might find it helpful to record important markers as you begin your keto weight loss journey.

Things like starting weight, starting measurements, and medical stats, like blood sugar and blood pressure, are noteworthy because they represent your starting point.

In addition to physical markers, you could also find it helpful to record your thoughts, feelings, goals, and plans in a journal. Writing down your short-term goals and tracking progress against them can motivate you to stay the course. Writing down how you feel at the beginning of your diet, then at regular intervals throughout, can help you self-assess and be aware of emotional highs and lows and how they relate to your milestones.

You might also consider keeping notes of things like favorite recipes or successful weekly meal plans. Jotting down what is working incredibly well for you and tripping you up allows you to plan and adjust using your discovery.

Finally, note your exercise and activity in your journal. You might underestimate or overestimate how active you are. Wearing an activity monitor, or making notes of how much exercise you are getting each week, can help you set activity goals that support your weight loss goals and your efforts to lead an overall healthier life.

Putting things in writing makes them more valid and more real, so consider journaling as much or as little as you find helpful as you travel this alternative path.

Toot Your Own Horn

Be intentional about celebrating your success. When you experience a win, whether it's a big or little one; stop, savor, and celebrate it. As you know, losing weight is not a piece of cake. Neither is keeping it off. Every pound lost represents hard work, dedication, and effort, so don't let that effort go unnoticed or unappreciated.

Celebrating your successes is a critical key to keep yourself motivated for the long haul.

Don't just celebrate each pound you lose, but also each behavior change you make, each unhelpful habit you break, and each new, healthy habit you establish.

Celebrate when you drop a clothing size or find yourself able to walk two miles instead of one, or when you discover you no longer need to ask for an extension for the seatbelt in airplanes.

Choose rewards that further support your efforts. Try to avoid rewarding yourself with food, but treat yourself to a bubble bath, a manicure, a new book, or a movie night with friends.

It's unnecessary that your milestone celebrations cost a lot of money.

Connections and Community

Having a strong, supportive community around you can help with any challenging task, weight loss included. Don't go it alone. Let those most closely connected to you know what you're doing and why. Ask for help and share your progress. Family members, friends, co-workers, neighbors; anyone you spend time with and are close to should be aware, so they can support you and not inadvertently sabotage you.

Besides letting those nearest and dearest to you in on what's happening in your life, take it one step further and find an accountability partner or a weight loss buddy. Having a go-to friend that will encourage you, celebrate you, and partner with you can be an enormous boost in keeping your motivation high.

Finally, consider searching out and joining a support group, either in person or online, with like-minded people. You might join a group of people following the keto diet specifically, or you might be more attracted to a group of 50-something losing weight on a variety of different plans. The secret is to find a group of people that can relate to you and support you just as you relate to and support them.

Be Positive in Your Thoughts and Actions

Did you know that research confirms that happier people make better decisions? And people who approach this endeavor with positivity and who confidently expect to succeed are much more apt to achieve the goals they have set for themselves.

With that in mind, remember that one effective way to keep yourself motivated is to talk positively about your weight loss and to verbalize out loud the positive steps you are taking to reach your goals.

Think positively about your weight loss experience and goals, and talk that way to yourself and others. Be realistic and pay attention to the actions you must take to achieve them. Don't just daydream or imagine you'll achieve your goals. Set small goals, then determine the action steps that will help you reach those goals, then visualize yourself following through on those steps as you make it happen. Cheer for yourself. Toss out that old way of thinking and any negativity that would pull you down, and embrace the good things you are doing for yourself.

CHAPTER 2:

TRICKS TO KEEP MOTIVATION HIGH

Prepare in Advance for How You'll Face Challenges.

This idea seems to contradict the previous point, to be positive in your thoughts and actions. While no one wants to run into roadblocks and challenges; the truth is, if it were easy to get the weight off and keep it off, we wouldn't have a society full of people challenged with weight management.

Stressors will arise, distractions will prove difficult, and circumstances won't always make it easy to stick to your plan. Finding ways to plan for how you'll handle those challenges and developing proper coping strategies will help provide the extra motivation you will need when times get tough.

Thinking ahead about birthdays, holidays, and special occasions like weddings, reunions, parties, and the like will help lessen the stress they can bring. Start brainstorming about these challenging times now, plan how you'll deal with setbacks and temptations when they come, and reach out to your weight loss buddy or family and friends to help you through those times.

Research shows that people who have healthy coping skills have a higher likelihood of reaching their weight and health-related goals and maintain a more beneficial lifestyle and weight long-term. So, think about the strategies you will incorporate into your new lifestyle. Maybe those strategies include:

- Exercising
- Taking up a hobby.
- Phoning a friend to talk it through.
- Changing your environment by going outside or into another room.

Keep in mind that you'll have a better chance of winning during those challenging times if you have planned how you will handle them.

Move Your Body

You might already be active and fit, or you might currently live a relatively sedentary lifestyle. No matter where you are starting in terms of fitness and activity, it's crucial that you understand that physical activity is an essential piece of the puzzle when losing weight and keeping it off.

Exercise helps you burn off calories, and it contributes to your overall health and well-being. What is the very best physical activity you can do to achieve maximum results? That's easy – it's the exercise (or exercises) that you enjoy the most! If you choose activities that you genuinely enjoy and are likely to stick with, you'll reap the benefits of getting more exercise.

Explore the many options and find things you enjoy to help you move your body more. You might find it motivating to join a class and exercise with a group or a workout buddy. Or you might find you need the solitude of working out alone so you can think, decompress, and focus on self-care. Crank up your favorite music, embrace those activities you will enjoy the most, and have at it.

Be Kind to Yourself

You've already read that being positive instead of negative is a big motivator and can help you reach your weight loss goals. But specifically, did you know that practicing kindness to yourself can also be a key indicator of your success?

Imagine you are dieting with a weight loss buddy. It's a dear friend that you are trying to encourage and support.

Let's say she has a rough day, falls off the wagon, and calls you in tears, confessing what she's done and beating herself up over it.

What do you say to her? Do you tell her you knew she'd stumble? That it was silly for her to think she could be successful this time since she's never been successful at reaching and maintaining her weight loss goals in the past?

Of course not! You encourage her, remind her she is human, and that all humans struggle sometimes. You ask her how you can support her, and you assure her she's able to reach her goals; that you're there to cheer her on every step of the way, and that you have full confidence in her.

It's easy to imagine supporting a friend in this situation, but it's a little harder to pay yourself that same courtesy and show yourself that same compassion. During this weight loss journey, being kind and forgiving to yourself is one of the most critical practices you can employ to stay motivated throughout your diet experience. Be your most passionate advocate, your head cheerleader, and your best friend.

Importance of a Good Hydration

The moment the body burns through your glycogen stores, you may feel the need to urinate more than glucose is flushing from your system. While these effects only last a few days, keeping yourself well hydrated will ensure you feel better during this transition.

Dehydration can often lead to symptoms such as headaches and muscle aches. To keep yourself in the best health, drink up loads of water and replenish your electrolytes.

Right Amount of Calories per Day

These are the basic guidelines for daily carbohydrates to consider as you blaze the path on the Ketogenic diet plan:

Ketogenic 0-20 Carbs is the scale used by physicians during its testing for epilepsy. It maintains the lowest level of carbs related to a restrictive medical diet. The patient is restricted from 10 to 15 grams each day—to ensure the proper ketosis levels remain, it must have a doctor's approval to keep your body functional and healthy.

Moderate 20-50 carbs are considered obese, have diabetes, or metabolically deranged; you will want to remain within these limits. Your body can achieve a ketosis state that supplies the ketone body. It is the theory used to calculate your meal plan.

Liberal 50-100 carbs are the best incentive if you're active and lean and attempt to maintain your weight.

As you now see, it is vital to experiment and categorize where you fall on the scales before you make any changes. As with any new diet changes, seek your doctor's advice. You will soon realize the keto diet is flexible—yet strict. Each individual will lose weight differently, and other people may not have the same goals as you. For now, as a beginner, you will use the second method.

Healthy Habits

Here is a list of simple exercises that people in their fifties and beyond can enjoy:

Light Weight Training

You can start with a little weight training to keep bone density and build muscle mass. If you're more interested in doing home exercises than joining the gym, invest in 2-pound weights and perform arm raises and shoulder presses.

Ideally, we recommend you join a fitness center or gym where you can meet like-minded folks. You can also get yourself a personal trainer who can guide customized workouts for you. Either way, remember to take it slow at first as you don't want to exert yourself too much.

Walking

If lifting weights isn't for you, good old-fashioned walking should also work for you. Consider taking a pleasant walk around your neighborhood or go to a park nearby. You'll be able to make some friends and enjoy the weather while you're at it too.

In case you'd rather workout at home, strap on a pedometer and get going around the house. The workouts will be available for you to get if you move your arms and lift your knees as you take each step.

Aerobics

Joining an aerobics class can significantly help you keep your muscles healthy while maintaining mobility. It will improve balance and reduce the risk of falls, thus drastically improving the overall quality of your life as you grow older.

Many studies have also shown how aerobic exercises can protect memory, sharpen your mind, and improve cognitive function among older adults. If you're not comfortable joining a class, you'll find plenty of videos online. Aerobic exercises have also got the heart pumping, improving cardiovascular help.

Swimming

Do you find regular exercise too dull? Swimming is a fun, affected-free exercise that can get you through the day. It's almost pain-free and won't trouble your aging joints. Swimming offers resistance training and will help you get back up to your feet again.

Here's how it works: the water offers gentle resistance while giving you a cardiovascular workout too. It also builds muscle capacity and helps you build strength again.

Yoga

What's not to love about yoga? It's relaxing, it's healthy, and you can enjoy it with a group. Yoga does an excellent job in improving flexibility in your joints. It allows seniors to remain limber and maintain their sense of balance. If you have trouble moving about or stretching, then you can try chair yoga.

Some classic yoga poses that you might want to try out include seated forward bend, downward-facing dog, and warrior.

Squats

When you're working on an exercise program, you shouldn't skip the idea of strength training. Squats happen to be an excellent way to strengthen the muscles of your lower body. Doing squats is relatively easy, and you won't need any equipment except for maybe a chair to support yourself. However, if you have trouble with balance, we suggest you skip this exercise and opt for something much more straightforward.

Sit-Ups

Sit-ups are a nice way to strengthen your core muscles, improve back pain problems and balance. Performing simple sit-ups should do the job. All you have to do is lie down on your back and keep your knees bent at an angle. Now place your hands behind your head and then gently try to lift your head. You should feel the sensation in your core muscles.

CHAPTER 3:

TECHNICAL ASPECTS

Important to Know During a Diet

There are keto diet laws that will help you meet your targets for weight reduction. A high-fat and low-carb eating plan, the Ketogenic diet, may be challenging to initiate. The fundamental rules that beginners should bear in mind before beginning the Keto Diet are provided below:

Rule #1: Must know foods to eat and avoid

You'll severely restrict carbohydrates by implementing a keto meal schedule and starting the day with between 20 and 30 grams (g) of carbohydrates.

Be sure you know what foods mainly include sugars, fat, and protein so that you can make the best decisions. It's not all pizza, spaghetti, popcorn, sweets, and ice cream; including carbohydrates, for instance. Beans can have protein, but they are substantial in carbohydrates as well. Carbs are often present in berries and vegetables. Meat (Protein) and pure fats such as butter and oils (including olive oil and coconut oil) are the other items that do not include carbohydrates.

Rule#2: Carefully think about your relationship with fat

People fear fat because they've been told it's going to kill them. On the usage of fat, there are several contrasting opinions. It gets confusing to know how precisely to consume them. It would also be useful to recognize that food is more than a single ingredient, and it is the general consistency of the diet that matters. Start making minor changes to what you consume every day, such as buying a sandwich on lettuce leaves and sub-green vegetables for fries, to plan for a high-fat diet, which may feel challenging at first. Then go for a non-starchy veggie instead of potatoes or rice for your dinner. With added oil, such as olive or avocado oil, start cooking. Realize the old dieting patterns don't make sense on a keto diet, so you won't get enough fat, such as having a primary skinless grilled chicken breast.

Nutritionists' plurality accepts that more monounsaturated fats, present in plant-based foods such as avocados and olive oil, should be consumed since they are known to be partially responsible for the heart-healthy benefits of the Mediterranean diet.

Rule#3: Change your view of Protein

Most of the keto diet's more popular myths are that you should consume as much protein based on your preferences. But the diet is not where you aim at carbohydrates.

You will need to maintain the consumption of protein moderate. It is essential to turn protein into glucose, so that overeating protein will bring the body out of ketosis. Think of the amounts, rather than the other way around, as a tiny piece of meat covered by a large quantity of fat.

Rule#4: Improve your cooking skills

Since too many things are off-limits, Keto causes you to eat more frequently at home. That's a positive thing since you don't know how many restaurants use oil or sugar. However, when you feed at home, you have a lot of influence on what goes into your meals. You ought to inform yourself with numerous keto-approved recipes, and selecting four to five recipes with ingredients that you know you'll enjoy is strongly recommended. You won't wait around asking whether to follow this direction and then switch to carbohydrates.

The keto diet is more about growing your calorie consumption, and most of us consume so many refined foods abundant in fat anyway. A diet like this helps you take out those items that can further decrease your excess weight and boost your nutrition.

While Keto takes out most big carbohydrates, you can take out refined carbs while also eating nutritious whole grains, such as brown rice and oats.

Rule#5: Bulletproof Coffee is a remarkable Keto drink

It is created in your coffee by mixing coconut oil and butter. This drink will help hold your appetite at bay, leaving your flexibility to prepare your next meal.

Just remember that coconut oil can raise LDL, or "poor" cholesterol levels, so you'll undoubtedly want to avoid this drink whether you have heart problems or are at an elevated risk for it because of family or personal health background.

Rule#6: Learn about the side effects—the Keto Flu and use fermented foods

There's one significant side effect you ought to be prepared for: the keto virus, given all the attributes of a Ketogenic diet (like weight loss). Keto flu is a word that applies to when the body is reacting to burning fat for energy when you start the diet. Certain persons have no trouble with it, and some are depressed. Your limbs may feel severely lethargic in the first week or ten days. Maybe going upstairs sounds unlikely. Perhaps you're struggling with emotional fog. Also, because of a shift in fiber consumption, Keto induces constipation or even diarrhea. For that reason, when your week is not wild with commitments and responsibilities, you can choose a start date; select a slower period when you can relax as required. In the same lines, you'll want to be careful to take things easy with exercise within the first week or two, when your body needs longer to change within the fuel to consume fat rather than carbohydrates.

Cutting out vital fiber sources, such as whole grains and fruits, will make you feel pretty backed up, so it's not a surprise that a widespread keto symptom is constipation.

Rule#7: Maintain a suitable level of electrolytes to save from Keto side effects

Your kidneys excrete more water and electrolytes during ketosis. Be sure that you get the sodium and potassium that your body requires to operate correctly. Salt the food, drink salted bone broth; and consume asparagus, kale, bell peppers, and arugula for non-starchy vegetables.

Rule#8: Increase your intake of the non-starchy veggies

Nutritionists say that Keto gets us to consume more non-starchy ones, such as broccoli, asparagus, and spinach because most adults don't get enough vegetables.

These vegetables help the digestive system provide the fiber it craves. And while most vegetables fill you up with fewer calories, there are also lower BMIs among people who consume veggies daily.

You can't always overdo things on the vegetables, as long as nutritionists are concerned, strive to provide at least one cup for any meal.

Rule#9: Intermittent fasting

In certain Keto circles, intermittent fasting is all the rage. It might sound drastic, but the most common therapies typically allow you to eat food for eight hours throughout the day. Your body gradually burns off all the carb reserves (i.e., glucose and glycogen) during fasting cycles and continues to consume body fat for energy.

Rule#10: Accept when Keto might not be right for you

Now that Ketogenic diets have become common, several keto hybrid diets, including variations focused on plants, have appeared. One is "ketotarian," primarily plant-based, but contains eggs, ghee, and fish and shellfish choices. You should be mindful about it since, on a Ketogenic diet, you should not consume beans or lentils, and because of their carbohydrate content, nuts and seeds are also limited. Therefore, you're only just left with some tofu, and you're going to have to focus on low-carb protein powder. There are also medical problems that may make you think twice before beginning keto or, before attempting it out, at least speak to the doctor. These involve persons on insulin and those on elevated blood sugar or high blood pressure oral and noninsulin injectable drugs. Also, dealing with GI difficulties may be an obstacle at the beginning. Constipation is one of the side effects of a Ketogenic diet, but if that's a problem, there's a severe excuse not to be on this very low-fiber diet. Finally, a Ketogenic diet may be too restrictive for you if current personal dietary limitations enable you to eliminate foods such as wheat, poultry, nuts, grains, or seafood. In another stringent diet, coming from a removal position will make things too challenging to obey.

Rul#11: Inform your family about your weight loss targets

Your strategy, inform them. During family dinners, you will not be willing to consume what they're consuming, so you'll want to brace them (and yourself) for what your new routines may look like. As this diet is mostly only carried out in the short term (three to six months), you should tell them that it is temporary.

If anyone understands the expectations on a keto diet, it does not harm because they are less inclined to force workplace snacks or propose sharing a side of fries while you're out for dinner.

Rule#12: We need to have a post-keto plan

A keto diet is not a diet that can last long. It's designed to be short-term. A couple of days each year, some individuals go on a keto diet; some may shed weight and improve their dietary patterns. Your overall aim should be "to shift your food to a healthy trend that requires consuming less wheat, less pasta, less rice, and less sugar," as well as, she notes, more non-starchy vegetables.

When the keto diet is done, think of what it would be like for you. Why can this temporary diet be used as a springboard to boost your long-term health?

Rule#13: A fatty breakfast

They go about their day attempting to adopt the plan, hit the evening, then remember they didn't get sufficient fat and drink thick cream to cover for it, whereas most people struggle at Keto. Instead, what you can do is fill as much of the fat as possible at "breakfast." Typically, that's coffee or black tea with one Tbsp. of butter, MCT oil, or ghee in it.

That's 15 g of fat if you have three eggs. Four pieces of bacon are around 15 g or so. Another 15 is half of an avocado. Each keto coffee cup is 14 g. In the morning, the target is to have at least one-third of the fat for the day because you don't have to think about it any later. You should measure the TDEE and work out the amount and then find out what 70 percent of it is in grams of fat. If your weight is 160 lbs. and you want to reduce to 150 lbs., you can have 150 g of fat all day long, and you can aim for at least 50 g for breakfast. If your weight is 110 and aims to hit 100, you can have 100 g of fat for the day and at least 33 for the breakfast shoot.

While most of the breakfast items we've seen are in the 15 g range of fat, we may make the regulation easier: split your target weight by 30, round it up, and that's how many "carb parts" you can get for breakfast.

A fat serving is:

- 4 slices of bacon
- 3 eggs
- Half of an avocado
- One tea or coffee with a Tbsp. of butter / MCT oil/ghee / heavy cream

Right now, this sounds like a lot of thought, but until you work out what your number is and look for a breakfast mix which you prefer, you don't have to worry again about it. Now, I'm looking forward to creamy, buttery java, and you're going to notice that you love the flavor, too.

Rule#14: One Fat per Meal

From your fatty meats and fatty breakfast, you can get much of your calories, but you always need to combine a little more to the meal to ensure you reach your target.

Adding cheese, salad sauce, or nuts is the best method to do this. You'll get the fat you like if you can have a handful of cheese, a handful of pecans or walnuts, or add 1 to 2 tsps. of olive oil and ranch dressing to your meal.

CHAPTER 4:

MACROS—WHAT ARE AND SUBDIVISION

Y ou can better understand how keto works by breaking down the components of the plan.

Explanation about Macros.

Macronutrients are what foods are made of. They are fat, protein and carbohydrates. Each type of macronutrient provides a certain amount of energy (calories) per gram consumed.

- Fat provides about 9 calories per gram
- Protein provides about 4 calories per gram
- Carbohydrates provide about 4 calories per gram

In the keto diet, 65 to 75 % of the food calories a person consume comes from fat. Estimation, 20 to 25 % should come from protein and the remaining 5 percent or so from carbohydrates.

Fats

One of the distinguishing marks of the Ketogenic diet is that, unlike some low-carb, high-protein diets that recommend moderate fat consumption, keto encourages exceptionally high fat-content. Most keto experts recommend that your diet includes 70%-80% fat, with only a reasonable amount of protein.

Ketosis can help contribute to both fat loss and weight loss, as it burns fat while reducing your feelings of hunger. When you're in ketosis, you need a diet low in carbs, high in fat, and a moderate amount of protein consumption to prime your metabolism for fat-burning efficiency.

Fats are not all the same. Some are simply better for your overall health than others. So, as much as possible, choose the healthier options.

Here are some great examples of healthy sources of fat.

- Nuts and nut butter: Nuts are not only high in fat but are also high in fiber and plant-based protein as well, making them satisfying and nutritious. Not all nuts are equal, either, so check out the nutrition composition of your favorites and enjoy a variety of nuts as snacks, toppings for your salads, or even as spreadable nut butter. Be mindful of added sugars in some nut butter.

- Seeds: Seeds like flax, hemp, and chia seeds are great fat sources. Hemp seeds are nutrient-dense and unique. These seeds are sometimes referred to as hemp hearts. These three types of seeds contain essential amino acids that you won't find in most plant-based protein sources.
- Eggs: You know already how versatile eggs can be, but did you know how nutritious they are? The egg yolk has antioxidants that support eye health and is rich in B vitamins.
- Avocados and avocado oil: Like eggs, avocados are so versatile you can easily use them differently every day of the week. Please don't be stingy with yourself with avocados because you'll get so many minerals, essential vitamins, fiber, and heart-healthy fats when you eat them. Avocado oil is a tasty drizzle on grilled vegetables and can make keto-friendly salad dressings and sauces.
- Olives and olive oil: If you're looking for a base for a marinade for meats, a dressing for salads, or a drizzle for vegetables, cold-pressed extra virgin olive oil is a brilliant choice. Olives and olive oil are rich in heart-healthy fats, contain vitamin E, and have anti-inflammatory properties. Delicious as a stand-alone snack and as additions to veggie wraps, salads, and omelets; olives are a keto favorite.
- Coconuts and coconut oil: Coconuts and coconut oil can help you achieve ketosis. They contain medium-chain triglycerides (MCTs), which your body can absorb quickly and burn as energy.
- Full-fat Greek yogurt: Yogurt has digestive benefits that make it worth the few carbs most full-fat varieties of Greek yogurt you'll find in the grocery store. It's a significant source of calcium, particularly important for women over 50, and a significant source of probiotics.
- Cheese: There are hundreds of cheese varieties available on the market, so you have a nearly endless selection at your disposal. Some cheeses offer different benefits than other types might, but all are high fat and low-carb. Whether you're adding cheese to your salads, soups, veggies, meat, or keto recipes, you'll find it to be a favorite in your new keto lifestyle.
- Butter: Of all the things on this list, this one might take the most time to wrap your head around. Butter has gained a bad wrap over the years, especially as fat-free and low-fat diets became popular.
- Fatty/oily fish: Fatty fish are rich in omega-3 fats, known for being heart-healthy; and high-quality protein. Anchovies, sardines, tuna, and salmon are examples of fatty fish.

Your mouth is probably watering by now after reading the benefits of all of these high-fat foods. While you might not have always thought of these fats as diet-friendly, but on keto, they are superstars and essential building blocks of your food plan.

Before covering how proteins and carbohydrates play into the keto plan, note these fats that should be limited or avoided.

- Fried foods: Sometimes, fried foods are the first things that come to mind when you think of high-fat foods. Some people will include deep-fried foods in their keto plans, but you need more information before deciding to what extent you will add them to yours.
- Artificial Trans fats: You can identify artificial Trans fats under the names "shortening" or "partially hydrogenated oils." You will find trans fats in cookies, cakes, pastries, and other highly processed snacks. They are known for significantly increasing heart disease risk. Regardless of the diet you are following, avoiding artificial Trans fats as much as possible should be your goal.
- Processed meats: It's best to make sure you keep your intake of processed meats like hot dogs, deli meat, salami, sausages, and cured and smoked meats to a minimum. While it might seem these meats with high-fat content would be a good fit and are even sometimes advertised as being keto-friendly, the truth is they should be limited.

Proteins

Fats are only one of the macronutrients that play an essential role in the Ketogenic diet. Protein is a vitally important component of all the cells in your body, and it is critically important to your daily eating plan and overall good health. Your magnificent body breaks down the proteins you eat into individual amino acids, and amino acids are critical to your tissues and muscles.

Protein serves many essential functions in your body. Here are a few.

- Muscles: The protein in your body helps with muscle growth and repair. Every day, your body breaks down and repairs the protein in your muscles. Your body relies on receiving a fresh supply of amino acids to help with muscle protein synthesis, creating new muscle mass.
- Bones, hair, nails, skin, and internal organs: Unlike in your muscles, where protein turnover happens daily, the process occurs at a slower pace in your bones, hair, nails, skin, and internal organs. But consuming adequate amounts of protein is no less critical, as these systems in your body also require new amino acids to replace those that are old and become damaged over time.
- Hormones: Many hormones in your body are proteins. Two big ones are insulin and somatotropin. Insulin, a hormone made in your pancreas, allows your body to use glucose, a type of sugar in carbohydrates, as fuel.
- Enzymes: An enzyme is a protein in a cell that creates chemical reactions in the body to help support life. Enzymes perform many important jobs for you, including breaking down food particles during the digestion process, destroying toxins in your system, and building muscles.

Many experts agree that eating adequate amounts of protein can help make weight loss and weight management more effortless. Eating protein can help with satiety by keeping you feeling fuller longer when compared to eating carbohydrates. Protein can prevent overeating because it triggers hormones to promote fullness and satisfaction, thus reducing appetite.

Here are some excellent options for protein sources for your keto diet.

- Meat: Meat is the first source of protein that comes to mind for many people. Things like chicken, turkey, grass-fed beef, pork, venison, elk, lamb, rabbit, and duck are good, filling animal protein sources.
- Seafood: In the section on fats, you saw that fatty fish is an excellent fat source. Did you know it's also a fantastic way to get protein in your diet? Nearly every type of seafood provides good nutrition and protein. Lobster, clams, crab, squid, shrimp, oysters, trout, snapper, grouper, mackerel, catfish, sea bass, cod, and tuna are just a few.
- Eggs and some dairy: You have already learned that eggs, Greek yogurt, and cottage cheese should be staples in your keto eating plan. They also contribute protein, making them serve multiple purposes. The secret to choosing keto-friendly dairy options, check the carbohydrates count on the nutrition label. Since some milk and cheese varieties have added sugars, they can be high in carbs, making them less friendly for keto dieters.
- Plant-based proteins: It can be challenging to find plant-based proteins that work with keto because nearly all plants contain some carbs, making it challenging to balance your keto macros.

Carbohydrates

Some say to keep your net carb intake to 20 grams or less per day, but most keto experts offer a range and recommend consuming about 15-30 grams of net carbohydrates every day. That's usually about 5-10% of your total calorie consumption.

What exactly does the term 'net carbs' mean? Net carbs are simply the carbohydrates that your body absorbs. With whole foods, you can calculate the net carbs by subtracting the fiber from the total carbohydrates. With processed foods, you subtract the fiber and the sugar alcohols from the total carbs.

Most people default to thinking about highly processed junk food and sweets when thinking of carbs. Those types of foods contain high carbohydrate counts, making them non-keto-friendly.

Pasta, potatoes, rice, and bread don't fall in the junk food category, but they are high-carb foods that you should avoid.

Here are some carbs that do work with keto.
- Olives: Olives were listed as a great source of fat, but did you know they have carbohydrates too? Since half the carbs in olives are fiber, they are a great carb source for your keto diet.
- Berries: Most fruits are very carbohydrate-rich, but berries are both low carb and high fiber, making them an excellent carb to choose when on a keto diet.
- Dark chocolate and cocoa powder: While you can't reach for a candy bar when you are following keto, that doesn't mean you can't enjoy the indulgence of some types of chocolate. Dark chocolate and cocoa powder are good sources of antioxidants. They contain nutrients that are good for your health and flavanols, which could lower your blood pressure, helping reduce your heart disease risk. Make sure you're choosing dark chocolate that has 85% or more cocoa. Dark chocolate with lesser amounts will usually have higher carbs and could disrupt ketosis. If you love chocolate, you'll enjoy the recipes in this book that use dark chocolate and cocoa powder. You can still enjoy the delicious chocolate flavor you love, even on this low-carb diet.
- Low-carb vegetables: Non-starchy vegetables like Brussels sprouts, broccoli, spinach, kale, cauliflower, and zucchini are high-fiber, low-calorie, low-carb options, making them excellent choices on keto. You can enjoy as many of these vegetables as you want on the Ketogenic diet.
- Avocados: You've already read about how amazing avocados are because of their high-fat content. They have all sorts of essential vitamins and minerals, including magnesium and potassium. For all that nutritional goodness, they only have two grams of net carbs, making them a top pick for your keto diet.
- Shirataki Noodles: These noodles consist of mostly water and fiber. They contain hardly any carbs, making them an excellent replacement for you if you miss eating pasta. They are most commonly found shaped like linguine, fettuccine, or rice and are available in many health food stores.

CHAPTER 5:

KETOSIS

What Is It?

When eating a high-carb diet, your body is in a metabolic state of glycolysis, which means that most of the energy your body uses comes from blood glucose. In this state, after each meal, your blood glucose is spiked, causing higher levels of insulin, which promotes storage of body fat and blocking the release of fat from your adipose (fat storage) tissues.

In contrast, a low-carb, high-fat diet makes the body into a metabolic being called ketosis—the body digest fat into ketone bodies (ketones) for fuel as its primary source of energy. Your body readily burns fat for energy in ketosis, and fat reserves are released continuously and consumed. It's a normal state whenever you're low on carbs for a few days. Your body will do this naturally.

Fats (fatty acids) and protein (amino acids) are essential for survival. There's nothing as a necessary carbohydrate. It simply does not exist.

Most of the cells in the human body use ketones and glucose for fuel. For cells that can only take glucose, like parts of the brain, the glycerol derived from dietary fats is made into glucose by the liver through gluconeogenesis.

The keto diet's primary goal is to keep us in nutritional ketosis all the time. For people who are just starting the keto diet, to be fully keto-adapted usually takes anywhere from four to eight weeks.

Once you become keto-adapted, glycogen (the glucose stored in your muscles and liver) decreases, you carry less water weight, your muscle endurance increases, and your overall energy levels are higher than before. Also, if you kick yourself out of ketosis by eating too many carbs, you return to ketosis much sooner than when you were not keto-adapted. Additionally, once you are keto-adapted, you can generally eat up to 50 grams of carbs per day and still maintain ketosis.

How Does It Work?

The Keto diet features a high-fat consumption (from 70 to 90 % of calories), a medium protein consumption (from 15 to 25 % of calories), and an extremely low carbohydrate consumption (from 5 to 10 % of calories).

Since the human body can work either by burning glucose or fat for energy, the Ketogenic diet, based on a reduction in carb intake, lets the body use fat as the primary source of energy and puts it in a metabolic state called ketosis. This happens when either dietary fat or stored fat is broken down, and the body begins to release molecules—ketones—that can be used for fuel.

So, you don't need to consume glucose to feel energetic and healthy. With the Keto diet guidance, you can replace carbohydrates with fat and protein, and get many benefits in your 50s. For example, it can help you decrease insulin and blood sugar levels, shed extra pounds and, moreover, power your brain. One more important thing: when insulin levels are stable, you always feel satiated because the insulin hormone doesn't need to alert the conscious brain that you're hungry.

Signals to Understand We Are in Ketosis

When you first start the keto diet, it's essential to know if and when you're in ketosis when you begin eating low-carb. Testing also lets us know that you're doing things right or wrong and whether you need to make any changes, and it is a great confidence booster.

An easy test is to sniff for "keto-breath." You might notice a somewhat fruity taste and a bit sour or even metallic after a few days. The reason for this? When the body is in ketosis, it makes the ketone bodies: acetone, acetoacetate, and beta-hydroxybutyrate. Acetone, in particular, is excreted through your urine and breath, which causes "keto-breath." This change in the smell of your breath and the taste in your mouth usually diminishes after a few weeks.

A way to tell is by using ketone urine test strips. They're relatively inexpensive and can instantly check the ketone levels in your urine. You can see them in packs of 100 for under $10 online or at most pharmacies. Try to take the test a few hours after you wake up in the morning because being dehydrated after a night's sleep can cause a false positive.

The most accurate test involves a blood ketone meter. This type of test is a bit pricier at around $40 for the meter and up to $5 per test strip. The upside is much more accurate because it tests your blood directly. For nutritional ketosis, your reading should be between 0.5 and 5.0 millimeters.

Long-term is not necessary to continuously check on your ketone levels. Within a few weeks, you'll know you're eating right, and it becomes very easy to stay in ketosis.

CHAPTER 6:

KETOGENIC DIET

What Food Based On

People complain about the difficulty of switching their grocery list to one that's Ketogenic-friendly. The fact is that food is expensive, and most of the food you have in your fridge is probably packed full of carbohydrates. It is why, if you're committing to a Ketogenic Diet, you need to do a clean sweep. That's right, everything that's packed with carbohydrates should be identified and set aside to make sure that you are not overeating.

Understanding the keto diet is the first step toward becoming a master at following the keto diet. By now, you recognize the critical role fats and proteins play in your new way of eating, giving you an excellent foundation.

How does eating a higher fat diet help you lose weight? Your body uses glucose as its primary source of energy. You obtain glucose when you eat carbohydrate foods. However, once you reduce your carbohydrate intake to the point that you deprive your body of glucose, it produces an alternative fuel source, called ketones, from stored fat.

Your brain is incredibly demanding. Because it's unable to store glucose, it expects a steady daily supply of about 120 grams. When you take in very few carbs, depriving your body of that daily supply of glucose, your system will first draw stored glucose from your liver. It will temporarily break down muscles and releases glucose.

After a few days of this, usually 3-4, your supply of stored glucose will become depleted enough that your insulin levels will start to drop. When that happens, your body will switch gears and begin to use fat as its primary source of fuel or energy. Your liver gets to work, producing ketones from fat. These ketone bodies start to build up in the blood, which is called ketosis.

Foods to Be Consumed in Moderation

Fats and Oils

Because fats will be included as part of all your meals, we recommend choosing a superb quality of ingredients that you can afford. Some of your best choices for fat are:

- Ghee or Clarified butter
- Avocado
- Coconut Oil

- Red Palm Oil
- Butter
- Coconut Butter
- Peanut Butter
- Chicken Fat
- Beef Tallow
- Non-hydrogenated Lard
- Macadamias and other nuts
- Egg Yolks
- Fishes that are high in Omega-3 Fatty Acids such as; salmon, mackerel, trout, tuna, and shellfish

Protein

Those on a keto diet will generally keep fat intake high, carbohydrate intake low, and protein intake at a moderate level. Some on the keto diet for weight loss have better success with higher protein and lower fat intake.

- Fresh meat: beef, veal, lamb, chicken, duck, pheasant, pork, etc.
- Deli meats: bacon, sausage, ham (make sure to watch out for added sugar and other fillers)
- Eggs: preferably free-range or organic eggs
- Fish: wild-caught salmon, catfish, halibut, trout, tuna, etc.
- Other seafood: lobster, crab, oyster, clams, mussels, etc.
- Peanut Butter: this is an excellent source of protein, but make sure to choose a brand that contains no added sugar

Dairy

Compared to other weight-loss diets, the keto diet encourages you to choose dairy products that are full fat. Some of the best dairy products that you can choose are:

- Hard and soft cheese: cream cheese, mozzarella, cheddar, etc.
- Cottage cheese
- Heavy whipping cream
- Sour cream
- Full-fat yogurt

Vegetables

Overall, vegetables are rich in vitamins and minerals that contribute to a healthy body. However, if you're aiming to avoid carbs, you should limit starchy vegetables such as potatoes, yams, peas, corn, beans, and most legumes. Other vegetables that are high in carbohydrates, such as parsnips and squash, should also be limited. Instead, stick with

green leafy vegetables and other low-carb veggies. Choose local or organic varieties if it fits with your budget.
- Spinach
- Lettuce
- Collard greens
- Mustard greens
- Bok Choy
- Kale
- Alfalfa sprouts
- Celery
- Tomato
- Broccoli
- Cauliflower

Fruits
Your choice of fruit on the keto diet is typically restricted to avocado and berries because fruits are high in carbohydrates and sugar.

Drinks
- Water
- Black coffee
- Herbal tea
- Wine: white wine and dry red wine are OK if they are only consumed occasionally.

Others
- Homemade mayo: if you want to buy mayo from the store, make sure that you watch out for added sugar
- Homemade mustard
- Any spices or herbs
- Stevia and other non-nutritive sweeteners such as Swerve
- Ketchup (Sugar-free)
- Dark chocolate/cocoa

Foods to Avoid

Bread and Grains
Bread is a staple food in many countries. You have loaves, bagels, tortillas, and the list goes on. However, no matter what form bread takes, they still contain a lot of carbs. The same applies to whole-grain as well because they are made from refined flour. Depending on your daily carb limit, eating a sandwich or bagel can put you way over

your daily limit. So, if you want to eat bread, it is best to make keto variants at home instead. Grains such as rice, wheat, and oats contain a lot of carbs too. So, limit or avoid that as well.

Fruits

Fruits are healthy for you. They are found to make you have a lower risk of heart disease and cancer. However, there are a few that you need to avoid in your keto diet. The problem is that some of those foods contain quite a lot of carbs, such as bananas, raisins, dates, mango, and pear. As a general rule, avoid sweet and dried fruits. Berries are an exception because they do not contain as much sugar and are rich in fiber, so you can still eat some of them, around 50 grams. Moderation is key.

Vegetables

Vegetables are healthy for your body. Most of the keto diet does not care how many vegetables you eat so long as they are low in starch. Vegetables that are high in fiber can aid with weight loss. On the one hand, they make you feel full for longer, so they help suppress your appetite. Another benefit is that your body would burn more calories to break and digest them.

Moreover, they help control blood sugar levels and aid with your bowel movements. But that also means you need to avoid or limit vegetables high in starch because they have more carbs than fiber. That includes corn, potato, sweet potato, and beets.

Pasta

Pasta is also a staple food in many countries. It is versatile and convenient. As with any other suitable food, pasta is rich in carbs. So, when you are on your keto diet, spaghetti or many different pasta types are not recommended. You can probably eat a small portion, but that is not suggested. Thankfully, that does not mean you need to give up on it altogether. If you are craving pasta, you can try some other low-in carbs, such as spiralized veggies or Shirataki noodles.

Cereal

Cereal is also a big offender because sugary breakfast cereals contain a lot of carbs. That also applies to "healthy cereals." Just because they use other words to describe their product does not mean that you should believe them. That also applies to oatmeal, whole-grain cereals, etc. So, if you get your cereal when you are doing keto, you are already way over your carb limit, and we haven't even added milk into the equation! Therefore, avoid whole-grain cereal or cereals that we mention here altogether.

CHAPTER 7:

MACROS INVOLVED PERCENT SUBDIVISION

Here are the same numbers broken down into an average 2000-calorie daily diet by grams and percentages:

2000-CALORIE DAILY KETOGENIC DIET

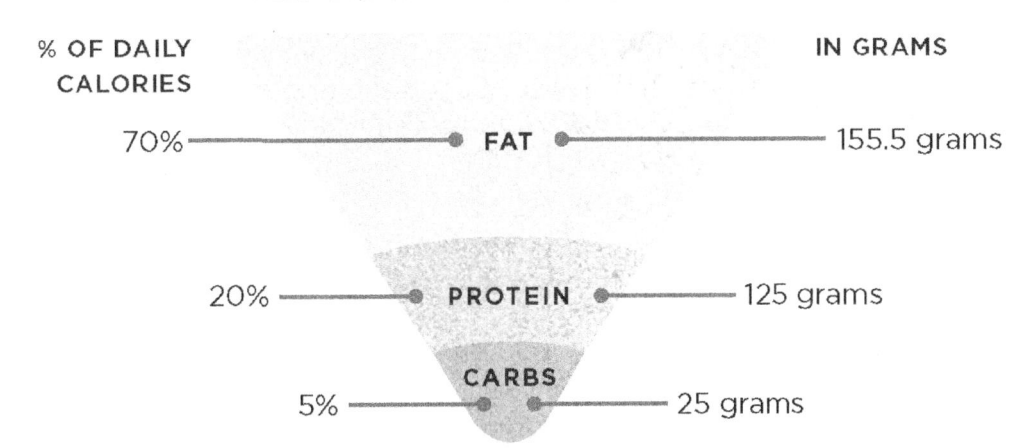

% OF DAILY CALORIES		IN GRAMS
70%	FAT	155.5 grams
20%	PROTEIN	125 grams
5%	CARBS	25 grams

Keep in mind that 2000 calories are just an example—the number of calories you consume daily should be tailored to your body, activity levels, and goals.

The number of calories you should eat depends on a few factors, including:
- Current lean body weight (total body weight minus body fat)
- Daily dose activity levels (do you work in an office, wait tables, compete as a professional athlete?)
- Workout regimen? If so:
- The types of workouts (weight lifting, cardio, or both)
- Hours per week of each type

Goal:
- Lose weight
- Maintain weight
- Gain muscle

There are many Ketogenic-based macro calculators available online, such as tasteaholics.com/keto-calculator and ketogains.com/ketogains-calculator. You can also find plenty of others through a quick Google search for "keto calculator." You'll be able to easily and quickly plug in your numbers and get an immediate estimation of your body's caloric needs.

One of the great things about the keto diet is that it's not necessary to track each and every number to hit your goals. Yet, if you want to track, it's a great way to speed up your progress, and tracking will give you a visual reminder to stay on the course every day.

Advantages of the Keto Diet and Benefits

If you're a person who's already celebrated your 50th birthday, that doesn't mean that your life becomes dull from here on, and you don't know how to spend your free time. Quite the opposite! You may often feel time-crunch because of work, family, and generally because of various life situations. Actually, it can be quite difficult to make time for yourself and, moreover, finding time to plan a healthy diet is more likely to be last on the list of your priorities. However, you can change your attitude towards your nutritional needs and move them to the top of that list when you find out all the benefits of a low-carb, high-fat diet for older people.

Improved Physical and Mental Health

With aging, you might notice an energy level drop due to different environmental and biological reasons. If you want to feel happy, active, and dynamic, pay closer attention to the Keto diet. Remember, reducing your carbohydrate intake usually leads to increasing your vital forces. When you start consuming a lower number of carbs, the body has to burn fat to fuel itself. This process causes fat synthesis and ketone production, i.e., breaking down accumulated fat for energy. In such a way, the low-carbohydrate diet can stimulate brainpower and positive changes in cognition (like improving memory and concentration).

Faster Metabolism

As already said in the previous section, older people have a slower metabolism. But thanks to the Keto diet, this problem can be solved. Excluding carb intake from your diet plan can help you to maintain healthy levels of blood sugar and, as a result, rev up your metabolism.

Weight-Shedding

It is no big secret that as a person gets older, shedding weight gets harder. People after 50 face the challenge of weight-loss for a variety of reasons (from increasing levels of stress, slower metabolic rate to rapid muscle loss). The struggle with excess weight may take a lot of time and effort for people over the age of 50. But there is a way out, and it is called the Keto diet.

This peculiar diet is highly effective for losing weight because it boosts the metabolism of fat, and the body itself starts shedding stored fat. As an added bonus, people who stick to the Keto diet get a reduced appetite, which helps to prevent over-eating and, thus, quicker weight loss. Unlike many low-fat diets, the Ketogenic one doesn't recommend you to track your calories or eat less. There's no need for that! Keto usually leaves you feeling full and satisfied after a meal.

Better Sleep

At old age, people tend to have trouble sleeping. A lot of people over 50 experience sleep disorders such as insomnia, sleep apnea, restless leg syndrome, and sleepwalking. People aged 50 and over should know that a long-term Ketogenic diet can have a positive impact on sleep. A significant reduction in carb intake and, at the same time, a substantial increase in fat intake create favorable conditions for a night of deeper sleep, eliminate certain sleep disturbance triggers, and make a person more energetic when the sun is up.

Protection from Age-Related Diseases

According to various scientific studies, the Keto diet can reduce the risks for specific age-related diseases, such as diabetes, different kinds of cancer, cardiovascular diseases, mental disorders, Parkinson's disease, multiple sclerosis, and fatty liver disease.

Common mistake and Issues

Even if you reach your 50s, that doesn't necessarily mean that you can't make a mistake, especially when starting something new like the Ketogenic diet. A lot of beginners, irrespective of age, make the same mistakes when following the low-carb diet. Check out the list of the top mistakes people often make and avoid them if you want to get brilliant results from such an effective diet.

- Inadequate Fluid Intake. On a keto diet, the body tries to burn more fat, and that's why it needs to be well-hydrated. Most people focus just on what they're eating and forget about what they're sipping. This mistake leads to a slower metabolism and, thus, halts weight-shedding. Besides, water is essential for nutrient circulation and flushing out toxins. So, if you're going to fasten your ketosis and improve your health, try to consume 3-4 liters of water (or even more) per day.
- Dairy Over-Enrichment. Remember, moderation is the key for you. Of course, you may find that dairy products are great for the Keto dieting plan. They're ideal high-fat and low-carb sources. However, don't forget that some dairy products contain sugar, and overeating them can destroy your dieting plan. Due to this, you need to calculate the dairy products' calories and pay attention to their nutrition labels.
- Lack of Fat. When it comes to the Keto diet, it means not just a low-carb, but also high-fat intake. At least 75% of the calories you consume should be provided from animal fats, monounsaturated fats, and olive oil. In such a way, you can ensure normal hormone function and boost your metabolism.

- Excess Protein Intake. In the previous section, we've drawn attention to the fact that if you eat too much protein, it'll cause adverse effects. Excess protein will be converted into glucose by your body and this can ruin your dietary needs.
- Not Preparing Yourself for 'Fat Adaptation'. It can be a bit time-consuming for your body to get used to burning off fat instead of glucose for fuel. So, you should prepare yourself and your body as well to experience the 'Fat Adaptation' or 'Keto Flu.' During the first week and even the second one, you may feel more fatigued, aches, and muscle cramps. That's pretty normal when your body adapts to another dietary need.
- Concealment from Your doctor. Think about your age... Your doctor has the right to know about every change in your life. And especially when it comes to nutritional changes. Talk to your doctor before including Keto products in your diet plan to make sure that this's a good idea for you and it won't harm your health.

Intoxication

It's crucial to drink plenty of water when beginning the keto diet. You may even notice that you're visiting the bathroom more often, and that's normal!

This happens because you're cutting out a lot of processed foods and have started eating more whole, natural foods instead. Processed foods have a lot of added sodium, and the sudden change in diet causes a sudden drop in sodium intake.

Additionally, the reduction in carbs reduces insulin levels, which in turn tells your kidneys to release excess stored sodium. Between the reduction in sodium intake and flushing of excess stored sodium, the body begins to excrete much more water than usual, and you end up low on sodium and other electrolytes. When this happens, you may experience symptoms such as fatigue, headaches, coughing, sniffles, irritability, and/or nausea. This state is generally known as the "keto flu." It's very important to know that this is not the actual influenza virus. It's called the keto flu only due to the similarity in symptoms, but it's neither contagious nor a real virus.

Many who experience these symptoms believe the keto diet made them sick and immediately went back to eating carbs. But the keto flu phase actually means your body is withdrawing from sugar, high carbs, and processed foods, and is readjusting so it can use fat as its fuel. The keto flu usually lasts just a few days while the body readjusts. You can abate its symptoms by adding more sodium and electrolytes to your diet.

How to Avoid

The keto flu is avoidable, and its duration can be reduced simply by adding more sodium to your diet. Here are some of the easiest ways to do it:

- Add more salt to your meals.
- Drink soup broths like beef and chicken.
- Eat saltier foods, like pickled vegetables and bacon.

Corrective Actions:

To replace other electrolytes, try to eat more of the foods listed below:

ELECTROLYTE	FOODS CONTAINING ELECTROLYTE
POTASSIUM	Avocados, nuts, dark leafy greens such as spinach and kale, salmon, plain yogurt, mushrooms
MAGNESIUM	Nuts, dark chocolate, artichokes, spinach, fish
CALCIUM	Cheeses, leafy greens, broccoli, seafood, almonds
PHOSPHORUS	Meats, cheeses, nuts, seeds, dark chocolate
CHLORIDE	Most vegetables, olives, salt, seaweed

CHAPTER 8:

TIPS FOR WOMEN OVER 50

Learn How to Count Your Macros

This is especially important at the beginning of your journey. As time goes on, you will learn how to estimate your meals without using a food scale.

Prepare Your Kitchen for Your Keto-friendly Foods

Once you've made a choice, it's time to get rid of all the foods in your kitchen that aren't allowed in the keto diet. To do this, check the nutritional labels of all the food items. Of course, there's no need to throw everything away. You can donate foods you don't need to food kitchens and other institutions that give food to the needy.

Purchase Some Keto Strips for Yourself

These are important so you can check your ketone levels and track your progress. You can purchase keto strips in pharmacies and online.

For instance, some of the best keto strips available on Amazon are:

Perfect Keto Ketone Test Strips, Smack fat Ketone Strips, and One Earth Ketone Strips.

Find an Activity You Enjoy

When you have done enough exercise, you will know what activities you like. One way to encourage yourself to exercise more regularly is by making it entertaining than a chore. If possible, stick to your favorite activities, and you can get the most out of your exercises.

Keep in mind that the activities you enjoy may not be effective or needed, so you need to find other exercises to compensate for, which you may not enjoy. For instance, if you like jogging, you can work your leg muscles, but your arms are not involved. So, you need to do pushups or other strength training exercises.

Check with a Healthcare Provider

Your dietitian can tell you whether a keto diet would work. Still, it helps to check in with your healthcare provider to ensure that you do not have any medical condition that prevents you from losing weight, such as hypothyroidism and polycystic ovarian syndrome. It helps to know well in advance whether your body is even capable of losing fat in the first place before you commit and see no result.

Hydrate Properly

That means drinking enough water or herbal tea and ditch sweetened beverages or other drinks that contain sugar altogether. Making the transition will be difficult for the first few weeks, but your body will thank you for it. There is nothing healthier than good old plain water, and the recommended amount is 2 gallons a day.

Supplements

When you get older, your body starts to lose its ability to absorb certain nutrients, which leads to deficits. For example; vitamin B12 and folate are some of the most common nutrients that people over 50 lack. They have an impact on your mood, energy level, and weight loss rate.

Have the Right Mindset

Our mindset is one of the very essential things you need to change when you've decided to follow the keto lifestyle. Without the right mindset, you might not stick with the diet long enough to enjoy all its benefits. Also, the proper mindset will keep you motivated to keep going no matter what challenges come your way.

Get Enough Sleep

Getting enough sleep helps your body regulate the hormones within it, so try to aim for 7 to 9 hours of sleep a day. You can get more restful sleep by creating a nighttime routine that involves not looking at a computer, phone, or TV screen for at least 1 hour before going to bed. You can drink warm milk or water to help your body relax, or even do 10 to 20 minutes of stretching to get a restful sleep.

Keep a Food Log

Add the calories and divide them into three to get an average. Now that you know how many you take, you can figure out how much you need to pay on average per day to reach your goals.

Tips for Women Over 60

Nobody told you that life was going to be this way! But don't worry. There's still plenty of time to make amendments and take care of your health. Here are a couple of tips that will allow you to lead a healthier life in your fifties:

Start Building on Immunity

Every day, our body is exposed to free radicals and toxins from the environment. The added stress of work and family problems doesn't make it any easier for us. To combat this, it's essential that you start consuming healthy veggies that contain plenty of antioxidants and build a healthier immune system.

This helps ward off unwanted illnesses and diseases, allowing you to maintain good health.

Adding more healthy veggies to your keto diet will help you obtain a variety of minerals, vitamins, and antioxidants.

Consider Quitting Smoking

It's never too late to try to quit smoking even if you are in your fifties. Once a smoker begins to quit, the body quickly starts to heal the previous damages caused by smoking. Once you start quitting, you'll notice how you'll be able to breathe easier, while acquiring a better sense of smell and taste. Over that period of time, eliminating the habit of smoking can greatly reduce the risks of high blood pressure, strokes, and heart attack. Please note how these diseases are much more common among folks who are in the fifties and above when compared to younger folks.

Not to mention, quitting smoking will help you stay more active and enjoy better health with your friends and family.

Stay Social

We've already mentioned this before but it's worth pondering on again and again. Aging can be a daunting process and trying to get through it all on your own isn't particularly helpful. We urge you to stay in touch with friends and family, or become a part of a local community club or network. Some older folks find it comforting to get an emotional support animal.

Being surrounded by people you love will give you a sense of belonging and will improve your mood. It'll also keep your mind and memory sharp as you engage in different conversations.

Health Screenings You Should Get After Your Fifties

Your fifties are considered the prime years of your life. Don't let the joy of these years be robbed away from you because of poor health. Getting simple tests done can go a long way in identifying any potential health problems that you may have. Here is a list of health screenings should get done:

- Check Your Blood Pressure

Your blood pressure is a reliable indicator of your heart health. In simple words, blood pressure is a measure of how fast blood travels through the artery walls. Very high or even very low blood pressure can be a sign of an underlying problem. Once you hit your 40s, you should have your blood pressure checked more often.

- EKG

The EKG reveals your heart health and activity. Short for electrocardiogram, the EKG helps identify problems in the heart. The process works by highlighting any rhythm problems that may be in the heart, such as poor heart muscles, improper blood flow, or any other form of abnormality. Getting an EKG is also a predictive measure for understanding the chances of a heart attack. Since people starting their fifties are at greater risk of getting a heart attack, you should get yourself checked more often.

- Mammogram

Mammograms help rule out the risks of breast cancer. Women who enter their fifties should ideally get a mammogram after every ten years. However, if you have a family history, it is advisable that you get one much earlier to rule out the possibilities of cancer.

- Blood Sugar Levels

If you're somebody who used to grab a fast-food meal every once in a while before you switched to keto, then you should definitely check your blood sugar levels more carefully. Blood sugar levels indicate whether or not you have diabetes. And you know how the saying goes, prevention is better than cure. It's best to clear these possibilities out of the way sooner than later.

- Check for Osteoporosis

Unfortunately, as you grow older, you also become susceptible to a number of bone diseases. Osteoporosis is a bone-related condition in which bones begin to lose mass, becoming frail and weak. Owing to this, seniors become more prone to fractures. This can make even the smallest of falls detrimental to your health.

- Annual Physical Exam

Your insurance must be providing coverage for your annual physical exam. So, there's no reason you should not take advantage of it. This checkup helps identify the state of your health. You'll probably be surprised by how much doctors can tell from a single blood test.

- Prostate Screening Exam

Once men hit their fifties, they should be screened for prostate cancer (similar to how women should get a mammogram and pap smear). Getting a screening done becomes especially important if cancer runs in your family.

- Eye Exam

As you start to age, you'll notice how your eyesight will start to deteriorate. It's quite likely that vision is not as sharp as it used to be. Ideally, you should have gotten your first eye exam during your 40s but it isn't too late. Get one as soon as possible to prevent symptoms from escalating.

- Be Wary of Any Weird Moles

While skin cancer can become a problem at any age, older adults should pay closer attention to any moles or unusual skin tags in their bodies. While most cancers can be easily treated, melanoma can be particularly quite dangerous. If you have noticed any recent moles in your body that have changed in color, size, or shape, make sure to visit the dermatologist.

- Check Your Cholesterol Levels

Now, we've talked about this plenty of times, but it's worth mentioning again. High cholesterol levels can be dangerous to your health and can be an indicator for a number of diseases; things become more complicated for conditions that don't show particular symptoms. Just to be on the safe side, your total cholesterol levels should be below 200 mg per deciliter. Your doctor will take a simple blood test and will give you a couple of guidelines with the results. In case there is something to be worried about, you should make serious dietary and lifestyle changes in your life.

EMILY ROSS

CHAPTER 9:

BREAKFAST RECIPES

1. Chocolate Protein Pancakes

Preparation Time: 10 minutes
Cooking Time: 15 minutes
Servings: 12 pancakes
Ingredients:
- 1/2 cup Almond flour, blanched
- 1/2 cup Whey protein powder - 1 tsp. Baking powder
- 1/8 tsp. Sea salt
- 3 Tbsp. Erythritol sweetener
- 1 tsp. Vanilla extract, unsweetened
- 3 Tbsp. Cocoa powder, organic, unsweetened
- 4 Eggs, pastured - 2 Tbsp. Avocado oil
- 1/3 cup Almond milk, unsweetened

Directions:
1. Place all the ingredients in a large mixing bowl, beat using an immersion blender until well combined, and then let the mixture stand for 5 minutes.
2. Then, take a medium skillet pan, place it over medium-low heat, grease it with avocado oil and pour in prepared pancake batter in small circles of about 3-inches diameter. Cover the skillet pan with a lid, let the pancakes cook for 3 minutes or until bubbles form on top, then flip them and continue cooking for 1 to 2 minutes or until nicely golden brown.
3. Cook remaining pancakes in the same manner, you will end up with 12 pancakes, and then let them cool at room temperature.
4. Place cooled pancakes in a freezer bag, with a parchment sheet between them, and freeze them for up to 3 months or store in the refrigerator for 5 to 7 days.
5. When ready to serve, microwave pancakes for 30 seconds to 1 minute or bake in the oven for 5 minutes until thoroughly heated.

Nutrition:
Calories: 237; Fat: 20 g; Protein: 11 g; Net Carbs: 5 g; Fiber: 2 g

2. Frittata

Preparation Time: 5 minutes
Cooking Time: 17 minutes
Servings: 1 frittata
Ingredients:

- 5 oz. Bacon slices, pastured, diced
- 1/2 Medium red onion, peeled, diced
- 1/2 Red bell pepper, cored, diced
- 1/4 tsp. Salt
- 1 tsp. Ground black pepper
- 3 Tbsp. Avocado oil
- 1/4 cup and 2 Tbsp. Grated parmesan cheese, full-fat
- 6 Eggs, pastured

Directions:

1. Take an 8 inches skillet pan, grease with oil, and place it over medium heat.
2. Add onion, pepper, and bacon, cook for 5 minutes or until slightly golden, and then season with salt and black pepper.
3. Meanwhile, crack the eggs in a bowl, add ¼ cup cheese and whisk until combined.
4. When bacon is cooked, pour the egg mixture into the pan, spread evenly, and cook for 5 minutes or until frittata is set.
5. In the meantime, switch on the broiler and let preheat.
6. When the frittata is set, sprinkle the remaining cheese on the top, then place the pan under the broiler and cook for 4 minutes or until golden brown.
7. Let the frittata cool at room temperature, then cut it into four pieces, place each frittata piece in a heatproof glass meal prep container and store them in the refrigerator for 5 to 7 days.
8. When ready to serve, microwave frittata in their container for 1 to 2 minutes or until thoroughly heated.

Nutrition:
Calories: 494; Fat: 40 g; Protein: 32 g; Net Carbs: 2.9 g; Fiber: 0.1 g

3. Bacon and Zucchini Muffins

Preparation Time: 10 minutes
Cooking Time: 35 minutes
Servings: 8 muffins
Ingredients:

- 2 cups Grated zucchini
- 1 Green onion, chopped
- 2 Thyme sprigs, leaves removed
- 1/2 cup Coconut flour
- 7 Eggs, pastured
- 1/2 tsp. Salt
- 1 tsp. Ground turmeric
- 5 Slices of bacon, pastured, diced
- 1 tsp. Baking powder
- 1/2 Tbsp. Apple cider vinegar
- 1 scoop Collagen peptides

Directions:

1. Set the oven to 350°F and let preheat until muffins are ready to bake.
2. Take a medium frying pan, place it over medium heat, add bacon pieces and cook for 3 to 5 minutes until crispy.
3. Then transfer cooked bacon in a large bowl, add remaining ingredients and stir until well combined.
4. Take an eight cups silicon muffin tray, grease the cups with avocado oil, and then evenly scoop the prepared batter in them.
5. Place the muffin tray into the oven and bake the muffins for 30 minutes or until thoroughly cooked and the top is nicely golden brown.
6. When done, take out muffins from the tray and cool on the wire rack.
7. Place muffins in a large freezer bag or wrap each muffin with foil and store them in the refrigerator for four days, or in the freezer for up to 3 months.
8. When ready to serve, microwave muffins for 45 seconds to 1 minute or until thoroughly heated.

Nutrition:
Calories: 104; Fat: 7.2 g; Protein: 7.9 g; Net Carbs: 1.5 g; Fiber: 0.9 g

4. Blueberry Pancake Bites

Preparation Time: 10 minutes
Cooking Time: 25 minutes
Servings: 24 pancake bites
Ingredients:

- 1/2 cup Frozen blueberries
- 1/2 cup Coconut flour
- 1 tsp. Baking powder
- 1/2 tsp. Salt
- 1/4 cup Swerve Sweetener
- 1/4 tsp. Cinnamon
- 1/2 tsp. Vanilla extract, unsweetened
- 1/4 cup Butter, grass-fed, unsalted, melted
- 4 Eggs, pastured
- 1/3 cup Water

Directions:

1. Set the oven to 350°F and let preheat until muffins are ready to bake.
2. Crack the eggs in a bowl, add vanilla and sweetener, whisk using an immersion blender until blended, and then blend in salt, cinnamon, butter, baking powder, and flour until incorporated and smooth batter comes together.
3. Let the batter sit for 10 minutes or until thickened and then blend in water until combined.
4. Take a 25 cups silicone mini-muffin tray, grease the cups with avocado oil, then evenly scoop the prepared batter in them and top with few blueberries, pressing the berries gently into the batter.
5. Place the muffin tray into the oven and bake the muffins for 25 minutes or until thoroughly cooked and the top is nicely golden brown.
6. When done, take out muffins from the tray and cool them on the wire rack.
7. Place muffins in a large freezer bag, or evenly divide them into packets and store them in the refrigerator for four days, or in the freezer for up to 3 months.
8. When ready to serve, microwave the muffins for 45 seconds to 1 minute or until thoroughly heated.

Nutrition:
Calories: 188; Fat: 13.8 g; Protein: 5.7 g; Net Carbs: 3.8 g; Fiber: 3.7 g

5. Pretzels

Preparation Time: 10 minutes
Cooking Time: 12 minutes
Servings: 6 pretzels
Ingredients:

- 1 1/2 cups Almond flour, blanched
- 1/2 tsp. Coconut sugar - 1 Tbsp. Baking powder
- 1/4 tsp. Xanthan gum - 2 1/4 tsp. Dry yeast, active
- 1/4 cup Water, lukewarm
- 2 Eggs, Pastured, beaten
- 3 cups Mozzarella cheese, full-fat, shredded
- 2 oz. Cream cheese, full-fat, cubed - 1 tsp. Salt

Directions:

1. Place yeast in a small bowl, add sugar, pour in water, stir until just mixed, and let it sit at a warm place for 10 minutes or until frothy.
2. Then, pour the yeast mixture into a food processor, add flour, xanthan gums, eggs, and baking powder, and pulse for 1 to 2 minutes or until well combined.
3. Take a heatproof bowl, add cream cheese and mozzarella, and microwave for 2 minutes or until melted, stirring every 30 seconds until smooth.
4. Add melted cheese into the processed flour mixture and continue blending until the dough comes together, scraping the mixture from the sides of the blender frequently. Transfer the dough into a bowl and then place it in the refrigerator for 20 minutes or until chilled. Meanwhile, set the oven to 400°F and let preheat.
5. Take out the chilled dough from the refrigerator, then divide the dough into six sections and shape each section into a bowl, using oiled hands.
6. Working on one section at a time, first, roll the section into an 18-inches long log, then take one end, loop it around and down across the bottom and loop the other end, in the same manner, crossing over the first loop to form a pretzel.
7. Prepare remaining pretzels in the same manner, and place them on a baking sheet lined with a parchment sheet.
8. Sprinkle salt over pretzels, pressing down lightly, then place the baking sheet into the oven and bake pretzels for 10 to 12 minutes until nicely golden.
9. When done, cool the pretzels at room temperature, then keep them in a large plastic bag and store in the refrigerator for up to a week or freeze for up to 3 months. When ready to serve, bake the pretzels at 400°F for 6 to 7 minutes until hot.

Nutrition:
Calories: 370; Fat: 28 g; Protein: 23 g; Net Carbs: 6 g; Fiber: 3 g

6.   **Breakfast Omelet with Mushrooms**

Preparation Time: 10 minutes
Cooking Time: 20 minutes
Servings: 1
Ingredients:
- 3 eggs, whisked
- 1 oz. butter, for frying
- 1 oz. cheese, shredded
- 2 Tbsp. yellow onion, chopped
- 5 small (4 big) mushrooms, sliced
- Salt and black pepper, to taste

Directions:
1. In a separate bowl, crack the eggs. Then add salt and pepper and whisk the mixture until frothy.
2. Melt the butter in a pan on medium heat.
3. Add the onion and mushrooms. Stir and cook for 5 minutes until the onion is translucent and the mushrooms are soft.
4. Pour the egg mixture into the pan and cover it with shredded cheese when the eggs are starting to become firm.
5. Fry until the eggs are almost firm.
6. Fold the Omelet in half and remove it from the heat.

Nutrition:
Calories: 510, Fat: 43 g, Protein: 25 g, Carbohydrates: 4 g

7. Morning Coconut Porridge

Preparation Time: 1 minute
Cooking Time: 5 minutes
Servings: 1
Ingredients:
- 1 egg, beaten
- 1 Tbsp. coconut milk
- 2 Tbsp. coconut flour
- 2 tsp. butter
- 1 cup water
- 1 pinch salt
- 2 Tbsp. flax seeds
- Blueberries and raspberries

Directions:
1. Put the flax seeds, coconut flour, water, and salt into a saucepan.
2. Heat this mixture until it has thickened slightly
3. Remove the mixture from the heat. Add beaten egg and put it on the stove again. Whisk slowly until you get a creamy texture.
4. Remove from the heat, add the butter, and stir.
5. Serve with coconut milk, blueberries, and raspberries.

Nutrition:
Calories: 486, Fat: 27 g, Protein: 15 g, Carbohydrates: 6 g

8. Sesame Keto Bagels

Preparation Time: 10 minutes
Cooking Time: 15 minutes
Servings: 6
Ingredients:
- 2 cups almond flour
- 3 eggs
- 1 Tbsp. baking powder
- 2½ cups Mozzarella cheese, shredded
- ½ cream cheese, cubed
- 1 pinch salt
- 2-3 tsp. sesame seeds

Directions:
1. Preheat the oven to 425°F.
2. Use a medium bowl to whisk the almond flour and baking powder. Add the mozzarella cheese and cubed cream cheese into a large bowl; mix and microwave for 90 seconds. Place 2 eggs into the almond mixture and stir in thoroughly to form a dough.
3. Part your dough into 6 portions and make into balls. Press every dough ball slightly to make a hole in the center and put your ball on the baking mat.
4. Brush the top of every bagel with the remaining egg and top with sesame seeds.
5. Bake for about 15 minutes.

Nutrition:
Calories: 469, Fat: 39 g, Protein: 23 g, Carbohydrates: 9 g

9. Baked Eggs in Avocado Halves

Preparation Time: 10 minutes
Cooking Time: 15 minutes
Servings: 2
Ingredients:
- 1 large avocado
- 2 eggs
- 3 oz. bacon
- 1 small tomato, chopped
- 1 pinch salt and paper
- ½ oz. lettuce, shredded

Directions:
1. Fry the bacon and cut it. Put aside.
2. Heat your oven to 375°F.
3. Cut the avocado into two halves and make a large hole in each half to place the egg in it.
4. Put avocado halves onto a baking sheet, place eggs, add salt and pepper. Cover the eggs with chopped tomatoes and bacon.
5. Bake for 15 minutes and top your avocadoes with shredded lettuce at the end.

Nutrition:
Calories: 810, Fat: 72 g, Protein: 26 g, Carbohydrates: 7 g

10. Spicy Cream Cheese Pancakes

Preparation Time: 15 minutes
Cooking Time: 20 minutes
Servings: 2
Ingredients:
- 3 eggs
- 9 Tbsp. cottage cheese
- Salt, to taste
- ½ Tbsp. Psyllium Husk ® powder
- Butter, for frying
- 4 oz. cream cheese
- 1 Tbsp. green pesto
- 1 Tbsp. olive oil
- ¼ red onion, finely sliced
- Black pepper, to taste

Directions:
1. Combine cream cheese, olive oil, and pesto. Put this mixture aside.
2. Blend eggs, Psyllium Husk ® powder, cottage cheese, and salt until the mixture is smooth. Leave it for 5 minutes.
3. Heat the butter in the pan and put several dollops of cottage cheese batter into the pan. Fry for a few minutes on each side.
4. Top your pancakes with a large amount of cream cheese mixture and several red onion slices.
5. Add black pepper and olive oil.

Nutrition:
Calories: 449, Fat: 38 g, Protein: 18 g, Carbohydrates: 7 g

11. Almond Flour Keto Pancakes

Preparation Time: 10 minutes
Cooking Time: 12 minutes
Servings: 10
Ingredients:

- 4 oz. softened cream cheese, at room temperature
- 1 medium-sized lemon, fresh zest (approximately 1 tsp.)
- 4 large-sized eggs, organic
- ½ cup almond flour
- 1 Tbsp. butter, for frying and serving

Directions:

1. Combine the almond flour with eggs, cream cheese, and lemon zest using a whisk in a medium-sized mixing bowl until combined well, and completely smooth, for a minute or two.
2. The next step is to heat a large, nonstick skillet over medium heat until hot. Once done; add 1 Tbsp. of butter until completely melted; swirl to coat the bottom completely.
3. Pour 3 Tbsp. of the prepared batter (for each pancake) and cook for a minute or two, until turns golden. Carefully flip; cook the other side for 2 more minutes. Transfer to a clean, large plate and continue cooking with the remaining batter.
4. Top the cooked pancakes with some butter; serve immediately and enjoy.

Nutrition:
Calories: 120, Total Fat: 8.6 g, Saturated Fat: 3.1 g, Protein: 3.9 g, Total Carbohydrates: 2 g, Dietary Fiber: 1 g, Sugars: 0.8 g

12. Keto Coconut Flour Egg Muffin

Preparation Time: 5 minutes
Cooking Time: 10 minutes
Servings: 2
Ingredients:

- 1 organic egg, large-sized
- 2 tsp. coconut flour or as required
- A pinch baking soda
- 1 Tbsp. coconut oil, to coat
- Salt, to taste

Directions:

1. Preheat your oven to 400°F. Lightly coat a large-sized coffee mug or ramekin dish with some coconut oil.
2. Using a fork; mix the entire ingredients together and make sure no lumps remain.
3. Bake for 10 to 12 minutes until cooked through.
4. Cut in half; serve immediately and enjoy.

Nutrition:

Calories: 48, Total Fat: 3.9 g, Saturated Fat: 1.1 g, Protein: 3.7 g, Total Carbohydrates: 1.7 g, Dietary Fiber: 0.3 g, Sugars: 0.5 g

13. Broccoli Cheddar Cheese Muffins

Preparation Time: 10 minutes
Cooking Time: 15 minutes
Servings: 6
Ingredients:

- 2/3 cup cheddar cheese, grated plus more for topping
- ¼ tsp. garlic powder
- ¾ cup broccoli, steamed and chopped (fresh or frozen and thawed)
- ¼ tsp. dried thyme

Directions:

1. Preheat your oven to 400°F. Combine the thyme with garlic powder in a large-sized mixing bowl until combined well and then, stir in the cheddar and broccoli. Evenly, divide the mixture into the muffin tins (with 6 cups), filling each cup approximately 2/3 full.
2. Sprinkle with more cheddar on top, if desired and then, bake until completely set for 12 to 15 minutes. Serve immediately and enjoy.

Nutrition:
Calories: 33, Total Fat: 4.2 g, Saturated Fat: 2.2 g, Protein: 2.2 g, Total Carbohydrates: 1.8 g, Dietary Fiber: 0.7 g, Sugars: 0.3 g

14. Chicken, Bacon, Avocado Caesar Salad

Preparation Time: 10 minutes
Cooking Time: 0 minutes
Servings: 4
Ingredients:

- 1 chicken breast, pre-cooked or grilled, sliced into small bite-sized slices
- 1 avocado, ripe, sliced in half, twist and discard the pit, remove the shell, and slice into approximately 1" slices.
- Creamy Caesar dressing (approximately 3 Tbsp. per salad)
- 1 cup bacon, pre-cooked, crumbled

Directions:

1. Combine the chicken breast with avocado slices and crumbled bacon between two large-sized bowls.
2. Top with a few spoonsful of the Creamy Caesar dressing; lightly toss the ingredients.
3. Serve immediately and enjoy.

Nutrition:

Calories: 322, Total Fat: 30 g, Saturated Fat: 8.6 g, Protein: 9.2 g, Total Carbohydrates: 5 g, Dietary Fiber: 3.4 g, Sugars: 0.9 g

15. Coconut Macadamia Bars

Preparation Time: 15 minutes
Cooking Time: 0 minutes + refrigeration
Servings: 6
Ingredients:
- ½ cup macadamia nuts
- 6 Tbsp. unsweetened coconut, shredded
- ½ cup almond butter
- 20 drops of stevia drops, preferably Sweetleaf ®
- ¼ cup coconut oil

Directions:
1. Crush the macadamia nuts using hands or in a food processor.
2. Combine coconut oil with the shredded coconut and almond butter in a large-sized mixing bowl. Add the stevia drops and chopped macadamia nuts.
3. Thoroughly mix and pour the prepared batter into a 9x9" baking dish lined with parchment paper.
4. Refrigerate overnight; slice into desired pieces. Serve and enjoy.

Nutrition:
Calories: 324, Total Fat: 32 g, Saturated Fat: 13 g, Protein: 5.6 g, Total Carbohydrates: 5 g, Dietary Fiber: 4 g, Sugars: 1.8 g

16. Macadamia Chocolate Fat Bomb

Preparation Time: 15 minutes
Cooking Time: 0 + refrigeration
Servings: 6
Ingredients:

- 2 oz. cocoa butter
- 4 oz. macadamias, chopped
- 2 Tbsp. Swerve
- ¼ cup coconut oil or heavy cream
- 2 Tbsp. cocoa powder, unsweetened

Directions:

1. Fill a large saucepan half full with boiling water. Place a small-sized saucepan over the large saucepan with the boiling water and melt the cocoa butter in it.
2. Once melted; add in the cocoa powder and then add the Swerve; mix well until the entire ingredients are completely melted and well blended.
3. Add in the macadamias; give everything a good stir.
4. Now, add the cream or coconut oil; mix well (bringing it to the temperature again). Pour the prepared mixture into paper candy cups or molds, filling them evenly. Let cool for a couple of minutes at room temperature and then place them in a refrigerator. Let chill until harden. Serve and enjoy.

Nutrition:

Calories: 267, Total Fat: 28 g, Saturated Fat: 15 g, Protein: 3 g, Total Carbohydrates: 3 g, Dietary Fiber: 2 g, Sugars: 0.9g

17. Keto Lemon Breakfast Fat Bombs

Preparation Time: 10 minutes
Cooking Time: 0 minutes + 50 minutes refrigeration
Servings: 6
Ingredients:

- 10 to 15 drops Stevia extract
- 1 Tbsp. lemon extract or lemon zest, organic
- 1 pack coconut butter or creamed coconut (approximately 3.5 oz.), softened
- 1 oz. extra virgin coconut oil, softened (approximately 1/8 cup)
- A pinch of Himalayan pink salt or sea salt

Directions:

1. Zest the lemon and ensure that the coconut oil and coconut butter are at room temperature and softened.
2. Combine the entire ingredients together in a large-sized mixing bowl and ensure the stevia and lemon zest are evenly distributed.
3. Fill each silicone candy mold or mini muffin paper cup with approximately 1 Tbsp. of the prepared coconut mixture and place them on a large-sized tray.
4. Place the tray inside the fridge and let chill until solid, for 40 to 50 minutes.
5. Keep refrigerated until ready to serve. Serve and enjoy.

Nutrition:
Calories: 184, Total Fat: 20 g, Saturated Fat: 14 g, Protein: 0.1 g, Total Carbohydrates: 0.2 g, Dietary Fiber: 0.1 g, Sugars: 0.1 g

18. Cheese Crepes

Preparation Time: 15 minutes
Cooking Time: 20 minutes
Servings: 5
Ingredients:
- 6 oz. cream cheese
- 1/3 cup Parmesan cheese
- 6 large organic eggs
- 1 tsp. granulated erythritol
- 1½ Tbsp. coconut flour
- 1/8 tsp. xanthan gum
- 2 Tbsp. unsalted butter

Directions:
1. Pulse the cream cheese, Parmesan cheese, eggs, and erythritol using a blender.
2. Place the coconut flour and xanthan gum and pulse again.
3. Now, pulse at medium speed. Transfer and put aside for 5 minutes.
4. Melt butter over medium-low heat.
5. Place 1 portion of the mixture and tilt the pan to spread into a thin layer.
6. Cook within 1½ minutes.
7. Flip the crepe and cook for 15-20 seconds more. Serve.

Nutrition:
Calories: 297, Total Fat: 25.1 g, Protein: 13.7 g, Net Carbs: 1.9 g, Total Carbs: 3.5 g, Cholesterol: 281 mg

19. Ricotta Pancakes

Preparation Time: 10 minutes
Cooking Time: 20 minutes
Servings: 4
Ingredients:
- 4 organic eggs
- ½ cup ricotta cheese
- ¼ cup vanilla whey protein powder
- ½ tsp. organic baking powder
- Salt
- ½ tsp. liquid stevia
- 2 Tbsp. unsalted butter

Directions:
1. Pulse all the ingredients in a blender. Heat butter over medium heat. Put the batter and spread it evenly. Cook for 2 minutes. Flip and cook again for 1–2 minutes. Serve.

Nutrition:
Calories: 184, Total Fat: 12.9 g, Protein: 14.6 g, Net Carbs: 2.7 g, Total Carbs: 2.7 g, Sugar: 0.8 g

20. Yogurt Waffles

Preparation Time: 15 minutes
Cooking Time: 25 minutes
Servings: 5
Ingredients:

- ½ cup golden flax seeds meal
- ½ cup plus 3 Tbsp. almond flour
- 1-1½ Tbsp. granulated erythritol
- 1 Tbsp. vanilla whey protein powder
- ¼ tsp. baking soda
- ½ tsp. organic baking powder
- ¼ tsp. xanthan gum
- Salt
- 1 large organic egg
- 1 organic egg
- 2 Tbsp. unsweetened almond milk
- 1½ Tbsp. unsalted butter
- 3 oz. plain Greek yogurt

Directions:

2. Preheat the waffle iron and then grease it.
3. Mix the flour, erythritol, protein powder, baking soda, baking powder, xanthan gum, and salt.
4. Beat the egg white until stiff peaks. In a third bowl, add 2 egg yolks, whole egg, almond milk, butter, yogurt, and beat.
5. Put egg mixture into the bowl of the flour mixture and mix.
6. Gently, fold in the beaten egg whites. Place ¼ cup of the mixture into preheated waffle iron and cook for about 4–5 minutes. Serve.

Nutrition:
Calories: 250, Protein: 8.4 g, Net Carbs: 3.2 g, Total Fat: 18.7 g

21. Broccoli Muffins

Preparation Time: 15 minutes
Cooking Time: 20 minutes
Servings: 6
Ingredients:
- 2 Tbsp. unsalted butter
- 6 large organic eggs
- ½ cup heavy whipping cream
- ½ cup Parmesan cheese
- Salt and ground black pepper
- 1¼ cups broccoli
- 2 Tbsp. parsley
- ½ cup Swiss cheese

Directions:
1. Heat the oven to 350°F, then grease a 12-cup muffin tin.
2. Mix the eggs, cream, Parmesan cheese, salt, and black pepper.
3. Divide the broccoli and parsley in the muffin cup.
4. Top the egg mixture with Swiss cheese.
5. Bake for 20 minutes. Cool for about 5 minutes. Serve.

Nutrition:
Calories: 231, Total Fat: 18.1 g, Protein: 13.5 g, Net Carbs: 2 g, Cholesterol: 228 mg, Sodium: 352 mg

22. Pumpkin Bread

Preparation Time: 15 minutes
Cooking Time: 1 hour
Servings: 16
Ingredients:
- 1 2/3 cups almond flour
- 1½ tsp. organic baking powder
- ½ tsp. pumpkin pie spice
- ½ tsp. cinnamon
- ½ tsp. cloves
- ½ tsp. salt
- 8 oz. cream cheese
- 6 organic eggs
- 1 Tbsp. coconut flour
- 1 cup powdered erythritol
- 1 tsp. stevia powder
- 1 tsp. organic lemon extract
- 1 cup pumpkin puree
- ½ cup coconut oil

Directions:
1. Heat oven to 325°F. Grease 2 bread loaf pans.
2. Mix almond flour, baking powder, spices, and salt in a small bowl.
3. In a second bowl, add the cream cheese, 1 egg, coconut flour, ¼ cup of erythritol, and ¼ tsp. of the stevia, and beat.
4. In a third bowl, add the pumpkin puree, oil, 5 eggs, ¾ cup of the erythritol, and ¾ tsp. of the stevia and mix.
5. Mix the pumpkin mixture into the bowl of the flour mixture.
6. Place about ¼ of the pumpkin mixture into each loaf pan.
7. Top each pan with the cream cheese mixture, plus the rest pumpkin mixture.
8. Bake for 50–60 minutes. Cool for 10 minutes. Slice and serve.

Nutrition:
Calories: 216, Total Fat: 19.8 g, Protein: 3.4 g, Net Carbs: 2.5 g, Cholesterol: 77 mg, Sodium: 140 mg

23. Eggs in Avocado Cups

Preparation Time: 10 minutes
Cooking Time: 20 minutes
Servings: 4
Ingredients:
- 2 avocados
- 4 organic eggs
- Salt
- Ground black pepper
- 4 Tbsp. cheddar cheese
- 2 cooked bacon
- 1 Tbsp. scallion greens

Directions:
1. Heat oven to 400°F. Remove 2 Tbsp. of flesh from the avocado.
2. Place avocado halves into a small baking dish.
3. Crack an egg in each avocado half and sprinkle with salt and black pepper.
4. Top each egg with cheddar cheese evenly.
5. Bake for 20 minutes. Serve with bacon and chives.

Nutrition:
Calories: 343, Total Fat: 29.1 g, Protein: 13.8 g, Net Carbs: 2.2 g, Cholesterol: 186 mg, Sodium: 372 mg

24. Cheddar Scramble

Preparation Time: 10 minutes
Cooking Time: 8 minutes
Servings: 6
Ingredients:
- 2 Tbsp. olive oil
- 1 small yellow onion
- 12 large organic eggs
- Salt and ground black pepper
- 4 oz. cheddar cheese

Directions:
1. Heat oil over medium heat.
2. Sauté the onion for 4–5 minutes.
3. Add the eggs, salt and black pepper, and cook within 3 minutes.
4. Remove, then stir in the cheese. Serve.

Nutrition:
Calories: 264, Total Fat: 20.9 g, Protein: 17.4 g, Net Carbs: 1.8 g, Cholesterol: 392 mg, Sodium: 285 mg

25. Bacon Omelet

Preparation Time: 10 minutes
Cooking Time: 15 minutes
Servings: 2
Ingredients:
- 4 organic eggs
- 1 Tbsp. chives
- Salt
- Ground black pepper
- 4 bacon slices
- 1 Tbsp. unsalted butter
- 2 oz. cheddar cheese

Directions:
1. Beat the eggs, chives, salt, and black pepper in a bowl.
2. Heat a pan over medium-high heat, then cook the bacon slices for 8–10 minutes.
3. Chop the bacon slices. Melt butter and cook the egg mixture for 2 minutes.
4. Flip the omelet and top with chopped bacon. Cook for 1–2 minutes.
5. Remove, then put the cheese in the center of the omelet. Serve.

Nutrition:
Calories: 427, Total Fat: 28.2 g, Protein: 29.1 g, Net Carbs: 1.2 g, Cholesterol: 469 mg, Sodium: 668 mg, Sugar: 1 g

26. Green Veggies Quiche

Preparation Time: 20 minutes
Cooking Time: 20 minutes
Servings: 4
Ingredients:
- 6 organic eggs
- ½ cup unsweetened almond milk
- Salt and ground black pepper
- 2 cups baby spinach
- ½ cup green bell pepper
- 1 scallion
- ¼ cup cilantro
- 1 Tbsp. chives,
- 3 Tbsp. mozzarella cheese

Directions:
1. Heat the oven to 400°F.
2. Grease a pie dish. Beat eggs, almond milk, salt, and black pepper. Set aside.
3. In another bowl, add the vegetables and herbs, then mix.
4. Place the veggie mixture and top with the egg mixture in the pie dish.
5. Bake for 20 minutes. Remove, then sprinkle with the Parmesan cheese.
6. Slice and serve.

Nutrition:

Calories: 176, Total Fat: 10.9 g, Protein: 15.4 g, Net Carbs: 4.1 g, Cholesterol: 257 mg, Sugar: 4 g

27. Chicken & Asparagus Frittata

Preparation Time: 15 minutes
Cooking Time: 12 minutes
Servings: 4
Ingredients:

- ½ cup grass-fed chicken breast
- 1/3 cup Parmesan cheese
- 6 organic eggs
- Salt
- Ground black pepper
- 1/3 cup boiled asparagus
- ¼ cup cherry tomatoes
- ¼ cup mozzarella cheese

Directions:

1. Heat broiler of the oven, then mix Parmesan cheese, eggs, salt, and black pepper in a bowl.
2. Melt butter, then cook the chicken and asparagus for 2–3 minutes.
3. Add the egg mixture and tomatoes and mix. Cook for 4–5 minutes.
4. Remove, then sprinkle with the Parmesan cheese.
5. Transfer the wok under the broiler and broil for 3–4 minutes. Slice and serve.

Nutrition:
Calories: 158, Total Fat: 9.3 g, Net Carbs: 1.3 g, Cholesterol: 265 mg, Sodium: 267 mg, Sugar: 1 g

28. Southwest Scrambled Egg Bites

Preparation Time: 10 minutes
Cooking Time: 23 minutes
Servings: 4
Ingredients:

- 5 eggs
- 1/2 tsp. hot pepper sauce
- 1/3 cup tomatoes
- 3 Tbsp. green chilies
- 1 tsp. black pepper
- 1/2 tsp. salt
- 2 Tbsp. nondairy milk

Directions:
1. Mix both the eggs and milk in a large cup. Add the hot sauce, pepper, and salt. Put small diced chilies and diced tomatoes in silicone cups. Fill each with 3/4 full with the egg mixture. Put the trivet in the pot and pour 1 cup water. Put the mold on the trivet. Set to high for 8 minutes. Cooldown before serving.

Nutrition:
Calories: 106, Fats: 7.4 g, Protein: 7.5 g, Carbs: 2 g

29. Bacon Egg Bites

Preparation Time: 10 minutes
Cooking Time: 22 minutes
Servings: 9
Ingredients:
- 1 cup cheese
- 1/2 green pepper
- 1/2 cup cottage cheese
- 4 slices bacon
- Pepper
- Salt
- 1 cup red onion
- 1 cup water
- 1/4 cup whip cream
- 1/4 cup egg whites
- 4 eggs

Directions:
1. Blend egg whites, eggs, cream, cheese (cottage), shredded cheese, pepper, and salt within 30 to 45 seconds in a blender. Put the egg mixture into mini muffin cups. Top each with bacon, peppers, and onion. Cover the muffin cups tightly with foil. Place the trivet in the pot and pour 1 cup water. Put the cups on the trivet. Set to steam for 12 minutes. Cooldown before serving.

Nutrition:
Calories: 124, Fats: 8 g, Protein: 9 g, Carbs: 3 g

30. Omelet Bites

Preparation Time: 5 minutes
Cooking Time: 8 minutes
Servings: 3
Ingredients:
- 1 handful mushrooms
- ¼ cup Green onion
- ¼ cup Green peppers
- 1/8 tsp. hot sauce
- Pepper, salt, mustard, garlic powder
- 1/2 cup cheese cheddar
- 1/2 cup cheese cottage
- 2 deli ham slices
- 4 eggs

Directions:
1. Whisk eggs, then the cheddar and cottage. Put the ham, veggies, and seasonings; mix. Pour the mixture into greased silicone molds. Put the trivet with the molds in the pot, then fill with 2 cups water. Steam for about 8 minutes. Transfer, cooldown before serving.

Nutrition:
Calories: 260, Fats: 16 g, Protein: 22 g, Carbs: 6 g

31. Cheddar & Bacon Egg Bites

Preparation Time: 10 minutes
Cooking Time: 8 minutes
Servings: 7
Ingredients:
- 1 cup sharp cheddar cheese
- 1 Tbsp. parsley flakes
- 4 eggs
- 4 Tbsp. cream
- Hot sauce
- 1 cup water
- 1/2 cup cheese
- 4 slices bacon

Directions:
1. Blend the cream, cheddar, cottage, and egg in a blender for 30 seconds. Stir in the parsley. Grease silicone egg bite molds. Divide the crumbled bacon between them. Put the egg batter into each cup. With a piece of foil, cover each mold. Place the trivet with the molds in the pot, then fill with 1 cup water. Steam for 8 minutes. Remove, let rest for 5 minutes. Serve, sprinkled with black pepper, and optional hot sauce.

Nutrition:
Calories: 167, Fats: 11.7 g, Protein: 13.5 g, Carbs: 1.5 g

32. Avocado Pico Egg Bites

Preparation Time: 15 minutes
Cooking Time: 10 minutes
Servings: 7
Ingredients:
Egg bites:
- 1/2 cup cheese cottage
- 1/2 cup Mexican cheese blend
- 1/4 cup heavy cream
- 1/4 tsp. chili powder
- 1/4 tsp. cumin
- 1/4 tsp. garlic powder
- 4 eggs
- Pepper
- Salt

Pico de Gallo:
- 1 avocado
- 1 jalapeno
- 1/2 tsp. salt
- 1/4 onion
- 2 Tbsp. cilantro
- 2 tsp. lime juice
- 4 Roma tomatoes

Directions:
1. Mix all of the Pico de Gallo ingredients except for the avocado. Gently fold in the avocado.
2. Blend all the egg bites ingredients in a blender. Spoon 1 Tbsp. of Pico de Gallo into each egg bite silicone mold. Place the trivet in the pot then fill with 1 cup water. Put the molds in the trivet. Set to high for 10 minutes. Remove. Serve topped with cheese and Pico de Gallo.

Nutrition:
Calories: 118, Fats: 9 g, Protein: 7 g, Carbs: 1 g

33. **Salmon Scramble**

Preparation Time: 10 minutes
Cooking Time: 5 minutes
Servings: 1
Ingredients:
- 2 smoked salmon pieces
- 1 organic egg yolk
- 1/8 tsp. red pepper flakes
- Black pepper
- 2 organic eggs
- 1 Tbsp. dill
- 1/8 tsp. garlic powder
- 1 Tbsp. olive oil

Directions:
1. Beat all items except salmon and oil. Stir in chopped salmon. Heat oil over a medium-low heat frying pan. Add the egg mixture and cook for 3-5 minutes. Serve.

Nutrition:
Calories: 376, Fats: 24.8 g, Protein: 24 g, Carbs: 3.4 g

34. <u>Mexican Scrambled Eggs</u>

Preparation Time: 5 minutes
Cooking Time: 10 minutes
Servings: 6
Ingredients:
- 6 eggs
- 2 jalapeños
- 1 tomato
- 3 oz. cheese
- 2 Tbsp. butter

Directions:
1. Heat butter over medium heat in a large pan. Add tomatoes, jalapeños, and green onions, then cook for 3 minutes. Add eggs, and continue for 2 minutes. Add cheese and season to taste. Serve.

Nutrition:
Calories: 239, Fats: 19.32 g, Protein: 13.92 g, Carbs: 2.38 g

35. Caprese Omelet

Preparation Time: 10 minutes
Cooking Time: 10 minutes
Servings: 2
Ingredients:
- 6 eggs
- 2 Tbsp. olive oil
- 3½ oz. halved cherry tomatoes
- 1 Tbsp. dried basil
- 5 1/3 oz. mozzarella cheese

Directions:
1. Mix the basil, eggs, salt, and black pepper in a bowl. Place a large skillet with oil over medium heat. Once hot, add tomatoes and cook. Top with egg and cook. Add cheese, adjust heat to low, and allow to fully set before serving.

Nutrition:
Calories: 423, Fats: 60.44 g, Protein: 43.08 g, Carbs: 6.81 g

36. Sausage Omelet

Preparation Time: 10 minutes
Cooking Time: 15 minutes
Servings: 2
Ingredients:
- ½ lb. gluten-free sausage links
- ½ cup heavy whipping cream
- Salt
- Black pepper
- 8 large organic eggs
- 1 cup cheddar cheese
- ¼ tsp. red pepper flakes

Directions:
1. Heat the oven to 350°F. Grease a baking dish. Cook the sausage for 8–10 minutes.
2. Put the rest of the ingredients in a bowl and beat. Remove sausage from the heat. Place cooked sausage in the baking dish, then top with the egg mixture. Bake for 30 minutes. Slice and serve.

Nutrition:
Calories: 334, Fats: 27.3 g, Protein: 20.6 g, Carbs: 1.1 g

37. Brown Hash with Zucchini

Preparation Time: 10 minutes
Cooking Time: 20 minutes
Servings: 2
Ingredients:

- 1 small onion
- 6 to 8 mushrooms
- 2 cups grass-fed ground beef
- 1 pinch salt
- 1 pinch ground black pepper
- ½ tsp. smoked paprika
- 2 eggs
- 1 avocado
- 10 black olives

Directions:
1. Heat-up air fryer for 350° F. Grease a pan with coconut oil. Add the onion, mushrooms, salt, and pepper to the pan. Add the ground beef, and smoked paprika, and eggs. Mix, then place the pan in Air Fryer. Set to cook for 18 to 20 minutes with a temperature, 375° F. Serve with chopped parsley and diced avocado!

Nutrition:
Calories: 290, Fats: 23 g, Protein: 20 g, Carbs: 15 g

38. Crunchy Radish & Zucchini Hash Browns

Preparation Time: 10 minutes
Cooking Time: 10 minutes
Servings: 6
Ingredients:
- 1 tsp. onion powder
- 1/2 cup zucchini
- 1/2 cup cheddar cheese
- 1/2 cup radishes
- 3 egg whites
- Pepper
- Salt

Directions:
1. Mix the egg whites in a bowl. Stir in the radishes, zucchini, seasonings, and cheese. Shape into 6 patties. Heat skillet over the medium-high setting. Grease. Cook the patties. Adjust to medium-low; cook for 3 to 5 minutes more. Serve.

Nutrition:
Calories: 70, Fats: 4.7 g, Protein: 5.5 g, Carbs: 1 g

39. Fennel Quiche

Preparation Time: 15 minutes
Cooking Time: 18 minutes
Servings: 4
Ingredients:
- 10 oz. fennel
- 1 cup spinach
- 5 eggs
- ½ cup almond flour
- 1 tsp. olive oil
- 1 Tbsp. butter
- 1 tsp. salt
- ¼ cup heavy cream
- 1 tsp. ground black pepper

Directions:
1. Combine the chopped spinach and chopped fennel in the big bowl. Whisk the egg in a separate bowl. Combine the whisked eggs with almond flour, butter, salt, heavy cream, and ground black pepper. Heat air fryer to 360°F. Grease. Then add the spinach-fennel mixture and pour the whisked egg mixture. Cook for 18 minutes. Remove, then chill. Slice and serve.

Nutrition:
Calories: 249, Fats: 19.1 g, Protein: 11.3 g, Carbs: 9.4 g

40. **Turkey Hash**

Preparation Time: 10 minutes
Cooking Time: 25 minutes
Servings: 5
Ingredients:

- 3 cups cauliflower florets
- 1 small yellow onion
- Salt
- Ground black pepper
- 1/4 cup heavy cream
- 2 Tbsp. unsalted butter
- 1 tsp. dried thyme
- 1 lb. cooked turkey meat

Directions:

1. Put the cauliflower in salt boiling water and cook within 4 minutes. Then chop the cauliflower and set aside. Dissolve the butter over medium heat in a large skillet and sauté onion for 4-5 minutes. Add thyme, salt, and black pepper, and sauté again for 1 minute. Stir in cauliflower and cook for 2 minutes. Stir in turkey and cook for 5-6 minutes. Stir in the cream and cook for 2 minutes more. Serve.

Nutrition:
Calories: 237, Fats: 11.5 g, Protein: 28.1 g, Carbs: 4.8 g

CHAPTER 10:

LUNCH RECIPES

41. Meatballs

Preparation Time: 5 minutes
Cooking Time: 3 minutes
Servings: 35 to 40 meatballs;
Ingredients:

- 1 1/4 lb. Ground beef, pastured
- 1/2 Medium white onion, peeled, minced
- 1 Tbsp. Minced garlic
- 1/2 tsp. Ground black pepper
- 1 tsp. Salt
- 1 tsp. Crushed red pepper flakes
- 1/4 cup Fresh rosemary, chopped
- 2 Tbsp. Butter, grass-fed, unsalted, softened
- 1 Tbsp. Apple cider vinegar

Directions:

1. Set the oven to 350°F and let preheat until meatballs are ready to bake.
2. Place all the ingredients in a bowl, stir until well combined, then shape the mixture into meatballs, 1 Tbsp. per meatball and place them on a baking tray lined with a parchment sheet.
3. Place the baking tray into the oven and bake the meatballs for 20 minutes, or until thoroughly cooked and nicely golden brown.
4. When done, cool the meatballs, then place them in batches in meal prep glass containers and refrigerate for up to 5 days or freeze for up to 3 months.
5. When ready to serve, reheat the meatballs in the oven at 400°F for 7 to 10 minutes or until hot.
6. Serve meatballs with zucchini noodles.

Nutrition:
Calories: 474; Fat: 21.7 g; Protein: 61.3 g; Net Carbs: 3.1 g; Fiber: 2.5 g

42. Rainbow Mason Jar Salad

Preparation Time: 10 minutes
Cooking Time: 30 minutes
Servings: 1 salad jar
Ingredients:
For the Salad:
- 1/2 cup Arugula, fresh
- 2 Medium radishes, sliced
- 1/4 Medium yellow squash, spiralized
- 1/4 cup Butternut squash, peeled, cubed
- 1/4 cup Fresh blueberries
- 1 Tbsp. Avocado oil

The Dressing:
- 1/4 Medium avocado, peeled, cubed
- 2 Tbsp. Avocado oil
- 1 Tbsp. Apple cider vinegar
- 1 Tbsp. Filtered water
- 1 Tbsp. Cilantro leaves
- 1/4 tsp. Salt

Directions:
1. Set the oven to 350°F and let preheat.
2. Then, place cubes of butternut squash in a bowl, drizzle with oil, toss until well coated, and then spread evenly on a baking sheet.
3. Place the baking sheet into the oven and bake for 30 minutes or until tender.
4. Meanwhile, prepare the salad dressing; and for this, place all the ingredients for the dressing in a blender and pulse for 1 to 2 minutes or until smooth, set aside until required.
5. When the butternut squash is baked, take out the baking sheet from the oven and let the squash cool for 15 minutes.
6. Then take a 32-ounce mason jar, pour in the prepared dressing, layer with radish, and top with roasted butternut squash, squash noodles, berries, and arugula.
7. Seal the jar and store in the refrigerator for up to 5 days.

Nutrition:
Calories: 516; Fat: 49 g; Protein: 2 g; Net Carbs: 6 g; Fiber: 6 g

43. Fish Cakes

Preparation Time: 10 minutes
Cooking Time: 8 minutes
Servings: 6 cakes
Ingredients:
For Fish Cakes:
- 1 lb. Whitefish fillet, wild-caught
- 1/4 cup Cilantro leaves and stem
- ¼ tsp. Salt
- 1/8 tsp. Red chili flakes
- 2 Garlic cloves, peeled
- Avocado oil – 2 Tbsp.

Dipping Sauce:
- 2 Avocados, peeled, pitted
- 1 Lemon, juiced
- 1/8 tsp. Salt
- 2 Tbsp. Water

Directions:
1. Prepare the fish cakes; and for this, place all the ingredients for the cake in a food processor, except for oil, and pulse for 1 to 2 minutes until evenly combined.
2. Then take a large skillet pan, place it on medium-high heat, add oil and leave until hot.
3. Shape the fish cake mixture into six patties, then add them into the heated pan in a single layer and cook for 4 minutes per side, or until thoroughly cooked and golden brown.
4. When done, transfer fish patties to a plate lined with paper towels and let them rest until cooled.
5. Meanwhile, prepare the sauce; and for this, place all the ingredients for the dip in a blender and pulse for 1 minute until smooth and creamy.
6. Place cooled fish cakes in batches in the meal prep glass containers and store in the refrigerator for up to 5 days or freeze for up to 3 months.
7. When ready to serve, microwave the fish cakes in their glass container for 1 to 2 minutes or until hot.

Nutrition:
Calories: 69; Fat: 6.5 g; Protein: 1.1 g; Net Carbs: 0.6 g; Fiber: 2.1 g

44. Lasagna Stuffed Peppers

Preparation Time: 15 minutes
Cooking Time: 1 hour and 5 minutes
Servings: 6 peppers

Ingredients:
- 6 Large bell pepper, destemmed, cored
- 1 1/2 lb. Ground beef, pastured
- 2 Tbsp. Minced garlic
- ¾ tsp. Sea salt
- ½ tsp. Ground black pepper
- 2 cups Marinara sauce, organic
- 1 Tbsp. Italian seasoning
- 1 cup Ricotta cheese, full-fat
- 1 cup Mozzarella cheese, full-fat, shredded

Directions:
1. Prepare the meat sauce; and for this, place a skillet pan over medium-high heat, grease with oil, then add garlic and cook for 30 seconds until fragrant.
2. Then add beef, stir well; cook for 10 minutes until nicely browned, season with salt, black pepper, and marinara sauce, stir well and simmer the sauce for 10 minutes. Meanwhile, set the oven to 375°F and let preheat.
3. When meat sauce is cooked, remove the pan from the oven and let cool for 5 minutes. In the meantime, prepare the peppers, and for this, cut off the tops, then scoop the inside seeds and ribs and slice slightly from the bottoms, without making any holes, so that peppers can stand upright.
4. Assemble the peppers, and for this, spoon 2 Tbsp. of prepared meat sauce in the bottom of peppers, then evenly top with ricotta cheese and mozzarella cheese, and add two more layers in the same manner with mozzarella cheese on the top.
5. Take a baking sheet, line it with aluminum foil, place the stuffed peppers on it, and then tent with aluminum foil.
6. Place the baking sheet into the oven, bake for 30 minutes, then remove the aluminum foil and continue baking for 10 minutes or until cheese melts and slightly browned. Cool the stuffed pepper at room temperature, then wrap each pepper with aluminum foil and store in the freezer for about 2 to 3 minutes.
7. When ready to serve, reheat the peppers into the oven at 350°F for 5 minutes or until hot.

Nutrition:
Calories: 412; Fat: 27 g; Protein: 30 g; Net Carbs: 8 g; Fiber: 2 g

45. Korean Ground Beef Bowl

Preparation Time: 10 minutes
Cooking Time: 20 minutes
Servings: 4 bowls;
Ingredients:
For Cauliflower Rice:
- 1 lb. Cauliflower, riced - 1/2 tsp. Sea salt
- 1/8 tsp. Ground black pepper - 1 Tbsp. Avocado oil

For the Beef:
- 1 lb. Beef, grass-fed - 1/2 tsp. Sea salt
- 2 Tbsp. Minced garlic - 1/4 cup Coconut aminos
- 1/4 tsp. Ground ginger - 1/4 tsp. Crushed red pepper flakes
- 1 Tbsp. Avocado oil - 2 tsp. Sesame oil
- 1/4 cup Beef broth, grass-fed

For the Garnish:
- 1/4 cup Sliced Green onions
- 1 tsp. Sesame seeds

Directions:
1. Prepare cauliflower rice; and for this, take a large skillet pan, place it over medium-high heat, add oil, and when hot, add cauliflower rice, season with salt and black pepper and cook for 5 minutes or until thoroughly cooked.
2. Then, remove the pan from the heat, transfer to a bowl, and set aside until required. Prepare the sauce; and for this, whisk together ginger, coconut aminos, red pepper flakes, sesame oil, and beef broth until combined, and set aside until required. Return skillet pan over medium-high heat, add avocado oil, and when hot, add beef; season with salt and cook for 10 minutes or until light brown.
3. Make the well in the pan, add garlic in it, and let it cook for 1 minute or until sauté, then mix it into the beef and pour in the prepared sauce.
4. Stir well and let beef simmer for 4 minutes or until sauce is thickened and not much liquid is left in the pan. Remove pan from the heat and let beef cool completely. Portion out the beef and cauliflower into four glass meal prep containers, garnish with green onion and sesame seeds, then cover with lid and store in the refrigerator for up to 5 days or freeze for up to 2 months.
5. When ready to serve, reheat the beef and cauliflower in its glass container in the microwave for 1 to 2 minutes or until hot.

Nutrition:
Calories: 513; Fat: 36 g; Protein: 35 g; Net Carbs: 9 g; Fiber: 3 g

46. Shrimp Lettuce Wraps with Buffalo Sauce

Preparation Time: 15 minutes
Cooking Time: 20 minutes
Servings: 4

Ingredients

- 1 egg, beaten
- 3 Tbsp. butter
- 16 oz. shrimp, peeled, deveined, with tails removed
- ¾ cup almond flour
- ¼ cup hot sauce (like Frank's)
- 1 tsp. extra-virgin olive oil
- Kosher salt
- Black pepper
- Garlic
- 1 head romaine lettuce, leaves parted, for serving
- ½ red onion, chopped
- Celery, finely sliced
- ½ cup blue cheese, cut into pieces

Directions:

1. To make the Buffalo sauce, melt the butter in a saucepan, add the garlic and cook this mixture for 1 minute. Pour hot sauce into the saucepan and whisk to combine. Set aside.
2. In one bowl, crack one egg, add salt and pepper and mix. In another bowl, put the almond flour, add salt and pepper and also combine. Dip each shrimp into the egg mixture first and then into the almond one.
3. Take a large frying pan. Heat the oil and cook your shrimp for about 2 minutes per side.
4. Add Buffalo sauce.
5. Serve in lettuce leaves. Top your shrimp with red onion, blue cheese, and celery.

Nutrition:
Calories: 606, Fat: 54 g, Protein: 33 g, Carbohydrates: 8 g

47. Poke Bowl with Salmon and Veggies

Preparation Time: 20 minutes
Cooking Time: 0 minutes
Servings: 2
Ingredients:
- 8 oz. raw salmon, skinless and deboned
- 1 Tbsp. sesame oil
- 1 tsp. tamari sauce
- 1 pinch salt
- 1 cup white cabbage, shredded
- 1 cup red cabbage, shredded
- ¼ cup cucumber, sliced
- 1 radish, sliced
- ½ avocado, diced
- ¼ cup cilantro
- 1 tsp. white sesame seeds
- 1 tsp. black sesame seeds

Directions:
1. To make the marinade, mix the sesame oil, tamari sauce, and salt. Set aside.
2. Cut your salmon into cubes and put it into a bowl. Pour the marinade over it.
3. Place the cucumber, red and white cabbage, radish, avocado, and cilantro into a bowl. Add the marinated salmon.
4. Top the salmon with white and black sesame seeds.

Nutrition:
Calories: 446, Fat: 34 g, Protein: 26 g, Carbohydrates: 11 g

48. Thai Cucumber Noodle Salad

Preparation Time: 10 minutes
Cooking Time: 1 minute
Servings: 3
Ingredients:

- 1 cucumber, cut into noodles
- Salt, to taste
- 3 pinches scallions, chopped
- 3 pinches raisins
- 3 tsp. sesame seeds
- ¼ cup unsalted almond butter
- 1 tsp. red curry paste
- ¼ cup canned coconut milk
- 1½ Tbsp. apple cider vinegar
- 1/8 tsp. coarse salt
- 1 Tbsp. coconut water

Directions:

1. With a Julienne peeler, make noodles from the cucumber.
2. To make the Thai peanut sauce, combine and mix thoroughly the unsalted almond butter, red curry paste, canned coconut milk, apple cider vinegar, coconut water, and add coarse salt.
3. Place your cucumber noodles over a spacious flat plate, pour ½ Tbsp. Thai peanut sauce over the noodles.
4. Top the cucumber noodles with chopped scallions, raisins, and sesame seeds.

Nutrition:
Calories: 132, Fat: 10 g, Protein: 3 g, Carbohydrates: 3 g

49. Wrapped Bacon Cheeseburger

Preparation Time: 15 minutes
Cooking Time: 8 minutes
Servings: 4
Ingredients:

- 7 oz. bacon
- 1½ lb. ground beef
- ½ tsp. salt
- ¼ tsp. pepper
- 4 oz. cheese, shredded
- 1 head iceberg or romaine lettuce, leaves parted and washed
- 1 tomato, sliced
- ¼ pickled cucumber, finely sliced

Directions:

1. Cook the bacon and set aside.
2. In a separate bowl, combine ground beef, salt, and pepper. Divide mixture into 4 sections, create balls, and press each one slightly to form a patty.
3. Put your patties into a frying pan and cook for about 4 minutes on each side.
4. Top each cooked patty with a slice of cheese, several pieces of bacon, and pickled cucumber. Add a bit of tomato.
5. Wrap each burger in a big lettuce leaf.

Nutrition:
Calories: 684, Fat: 51 g, Protein: 48 g, Carbohydrates: 5 g

50. Hearty Lunch Salad with Broccoli and Bacon

Preparation Time: 10 minutes
Cooking Time: 10 minutes
Servings: 5
Ingredients:
- 4 cups broccoli florets, chopped
- 7 slices bacon, fried and crumbled
- ¼ cup red onion, diced
- ¼ cup almonds, sliced
- ½ cup mayo
- ¼ cup sour cream
- 1 tsp. white distilled vinegar
- Salt
- 6 oz. cheddar, cut into small cubes

Directions:
1. In a mixing bowl, combine the cheddar, broccoli, bacon, almonds, and onion. Stir these ingredients thoroughly.
2. In another bowl, combine the sour cream, mayo, vinegar, and salt. Stir the ingredients well and pour this mixture over your broccoli salad.

Nutrition:
Calories: 267, Fat: 20 g, Protein: 12 g, Carbohydrates: 7 g

51. Fatty Burger Bombs

Preparation Time: 15 minutes
Cooking Time: 15 minutes
Servings: 20
Ingredients:
- 1 lb. ground beef
- ½ tsp. garlic powder
- Kosher salt and black pepper
- 1 oz. cold butter, cut into 20 pieces
- ½ block cheddar cheese, cut into 20 pieces

Directions:
1. Preheat the oven to 375°F.
2. In a separate bowl, mix the ground beef, garlic powder, salt, and pepper.
3. Use a mini muffin tin to form your bombs.
4. Put about 1 Tbsp. of beef into each muffin tin cup. Make sure that you completely cover the bottom.
5. Add a piece of butter on top and put 1 Tbsp. of beef over the butter.
6. Place a piece of cheese on the top and put the remaining beef over the cheese.
7. Bake your bombs for about 15 minutes.

Nutrition:
Calories: 80, Fat: 7 g, Protein: 5 g, Carbohydrates: 0 g

52. Avocado Taco

Preparation Time: 10 minutes
Cooking Time: 15 minutes
Servings: 6
Ingredients:
- 1 lb. ground beef
- 3 avocado, halved
- 1 Tbsp. Chili powder
- ½ tsp. salt
- ¾ tsp. cumin
- ½ tsp. oregano, dried
- ¼ tsp. garlic powder
- ¼ tsp. onion powder
- 8 Tbsp. tomato sauce
- 1 cup cheddar cheese, shredded
- ¼ cup cherry tomatoes, sliced
- ¼ cup lettuce, shredded
- ½ cup sour cream

Directions:
1. Pit halved avocados. Set aside.
2. Place the ground beef into a saucepan. Cook over medium heat until it is browned. Add the seasoning and tomato sauce. Stir well and cook for about 4 minutes.
3. Load each avocado half with the beef.
4. Top with shredded cheese and lettuce, tomato slices, and sour cream.

Nutrition:
Calories: 278, Fat: 22 g, Protein: 18 g, Carbohydrates: 2 g

53. <u>Chicken Quesadillas</u>

Preparation Time: 10 minutes
Cooking Time: 15 minutes
Servings: 2
Ingredients:
- 1½ cups Mozzarella cheese, shredded
- 1½ cups Cheddar cheese, shredded
- 1 cup chicken, cooked and shredded
- 1 bell pepper, sliced
- ¼ cup tomato, diced
- 1/8 cup green onion
- 1 Tbsp. extra-virgin olive oil

Directions:
1. Preheat the oven to 400°F. Use parchment paper to cover a pizza pan.
2. Combine your cheeses and bake the cheese shell for about 5 minutes.
3. Put the chicken on one-half of the cheese shell. Add peppers, tomatoes, green onion, and fold your shell in half over the fillings.
4. Return your folded cheese shell to the oven again for 4-5 minutes.

Nutrients:
Calories: 599, Fat: 40.5 g, Protein: 52.7 g, Carbohydrates: 6.1 g

54. Salmon Sushi Rolls

Preparation Time: 15 minutes
Cooking Time: 15 minutes
Servings: 5 (4 pieces each)
Ingredients:
- 4 oz. smoked salmon
- ¼ red bell pepper, cut into matchstick pieces
- ½ cucumber, cut into matchstick pieces
- ½ avocado
- 20 seaweed sheets
- ½ cup Water

Directions:
1. Cut the salmon and avocado the same way that you cut the red pepper and cucumber.
2. Place seaweed snacks on a cutting board. Put a cup of water nearby. Wet your fingers with water and wet one edge of each seaweed sheet.
3. Put one piece of salmon, pepper, cucumber, and avocado on each seaweed snack and roll them up.

Calories: 320, Fat: 20 g, Protein: 24 g, Carbohydrates: 8 g

55. Mediterranean Salad with Grilled Chicken

Preparation Time: 15-30 minutes
Cooking Time: 15 minutes
Servings: 4
Ingredients:
- 4 romaine lettuce leaves, washed and dried
- 1 cucumber, diced
- 2 tomatoes, diced
- 1 red onion, sliced
- 1 avocado, sliced
- 1/3 cup Kalamata olives, pitted and chopped
- 2 Tbsp. olive oil
- ¼ cup lemon juice
- 2 Tbsp. water
- 2 Tbsp. red wine vinegar
- 2 Tbsp. parsley, chopped
- 2 Tbsp. basil, dried
- 2 Tbsp. garlic, chopped
- 1 tsp. oregano, dried
- 1 tsp. salt
- Black pepper, to taste
- 1 lb. chicken fillets

Directions:
1. To make the marinade, mix the olive oil, lemon juice, water, red wine vinegar, parsley, basil, oregano, salt, and pepper. Divide the marinade into two halves.
2. Place the chicken into the marinade for 15-30 minutes.
3. In a separate bowl combine the lettuce leaves, cucumber, tomatoes, onion, avocado, and olives. Stir well.
4. Pour 1 Tbsp. of oil into a pan and grill the chicken until it is browned on both sides. Slice your chicken and add it to the salad.
5. Sprinkle your salad with the remaining marinade.

Nutrition:
Calories: 336, Fat: 21 g, Protein: 24 g, Carbohydrates: 13 g

56. Creamy Cauliflower Soup

Preparation Time: 10 minutes
Cooking Time: 40 minutes
Servings: 5
Ingredients:

- 21 head cauliflower, cut into florets
- 3 Tbsp. olive oil
- ¾ tsp. sea salt
- 4 cloves garlic
- 1 Tbsp. thyme, fresh
- 4 cups chicken broth
- 8 oz. cream cheese, cut into cubes
- ¼ tsp. black pepper
- 1/8 cup Green onion, chopped
- 1/8 cup Parsley, chopped

Directions:

Preheat the oven to 425°F. Place the cauliflower florets into a bowl. Add 2 Tbsp. of olive oil over them and ¼ tsp of sea salt. Bake for about 30 minutes in the oven.

Place the remaining olive oil in a pot, add the garlic and thyme and sauté for 1 minute. Pour the chicken broth and baked cauliflower into the pot. Boil for 5-10 minutes. Add the cream cheese and mix the soup with an immersion blender. Top with green onion and parsley.

Nutrition:

Carbohydrates: 12 g, Fat: 24 g, Protein: 6 g, Calories: 286

57. **Easy Keto Smoked Salmon Lunch Bowl**

Preparation Time: 15 minutes
Cooking Time: 0 minutes
Servings: 2
Ingredients:

- 12 oz. smoked salmon
- 4 Tbsp. mayonnaise
- 2 oz. spinach
- 1 Tbsp. olive oil
- 1 medium lime
- Pepper
- Salt

Directions:

1. Arrange the mayonnaise, salmon, and spinach on a plate. Sprinkle olive oil over the spinach.
2. Serve with lime wedges and put salt and pepper.

Nutrition:
Calories: 457, Fats: 34.8 g, Protein: 32.3 g, Net Carbs: 1.9 g

58. Easy One-Pan Ground Beef and Green Beans

Preparation Time: 15 minutes
Cooking Time: 15 minutes
Servings: 2
Ingredients:
- 10 oz. ground beef
- 9 oz. green beans
- Pepper
- Salt
- 2 Tbsp. sour cream
- 3½ oz. butter

Directions:
1. Heat the butter into a pan over high heat.
2. Put the ground beef, the pepper, and salt. Cook.
3. Reduce heat to medium. Add the remaining butter and the green beans, then cook within five minutes. Put pepper and salt, then transfer. Serve with a dollop of sour cream.

Nutrition:
Calories: 787.5, Fats: 71.75 g, Protein: 27.5 g Net Carbs: 6.65 g

59. Easy Spinach and Bacon Salad

Preparation Time: 15 minutes
Cooking Time: 15 minutes
Servings: 4
Ingredients:
- 8 oz. spinach
- 4 large hard-boiled eggs
- 6 oz. bacon
- 2 medium red onions
- 2 cups of mayonnaise
- Pepper
- Salt

Directions:
1. Cook the bacon, then chop into pieces. Set aside.
2. Slice the hard-boiled eggs, and then rinse the spinach.
3. Combine the spinach, mayonnaise, and bacon fat into a large cup, put pepper and salt.
4. Add the red onion, sliced eggs, and bacon into the salad, then toss. Serve.

Nutrition:
Calories: 509.15, Fats: 45.9 g, Protein: 19.75 g, Net Carbs: 2.5 g

60. Easy Keto Italian Plate

Preparation Time: 15 minutes
Cooking Time: 0 minutes
Servings: 2
Ingredients:
- 7 oz. mozzarella cheese
- 7 oz. prosciutto
- 2 tomatoes
- 4 Tbsp. olive oil
- 10 whole green olives
- Pepper
- Salt

Directions:
1. Arrange the tomato, olives, mozzarella, and prosciutto on a plate.
2. Season the tomato and cheese with pepper and salt. Serve with olive oil.

Nutrition:
Calories: 780.98, Fats: 60.74 g, Protein: 50.87 g, Net Carbs: 5.9 g

61. Fresh Broccoli and Dill Keto Salad

Preparation Time: 15 minutes
Cooking Time: 7 minutes
Servings: 3
Ingredients:
- 16 oz. broccoli
- ½ cup mayonnaise
- ¾ cup chopped dill
- Salt
- Pepper

Directions:
1. Boil salted water in a saucepan. Put the chopped broccoli in the pot and boil for 3-5 minutes. Drain and set aside. Once cooled, mix the rest of the ingredients. Put pepper and salt, then serve.

Nutrition:
Calories: 303.33, Fats: 28.1 g, Protein: 4.03 g, Net Carbs: 6.2 g,

62. Keto Smoked Salmon Filled Avocados

Preparation Time: 15 minutes
Cooking Time: 0 minutes
Servings: 1
Ingredients:
- 1 avocado
- 3 oz. smoked salmon
- 4 Tbsp. sour cream
- 1 Tbsp. lemon juice
- Pepper
- Salt

Directions:
1. Cut the avocado into two. Place the sour cream in the hollow parts of the avocado with smoked salmon. Put pepper and salt, squeeze lemon juice over the top. Serve.

Nutrition:
Calories: 517, Fats: 42.6 g, Protein: 20.6 g, Net Carbs: 6.7 g

63. Low-Carb Broccoli Lemon Parmesan Soup

Preparation Time: 15 minutes
Cooking Time: 15 minutes
Servings: 4
Ingredients:

- 3 cups water
- 1 cup unsweetened almond milk
- 32 oz. broccoli florets
- 1 cup heavy whipping cream
- ¾ cup Parmesan cheese
- Salt
- Pepper
- 2 Tbsp. lemon juice

Directions:

1. Cook the broccoli with water over medium-high heat.
2. Take out 1 cup of the cooking liquid, and remove the rest.
3. Blend half the broccoli, reserved cooking oil, unsweetened almond milk, heavy cream, and salt plus pepper in a blender.
4. Put the blended items to the remaining broccoli, and stir with parmesan cheese and lemon juice. Cook until heated through. Serve with parmesan cheese on the top.

Nutrition:
Calories: 371, Fats: 28.38 g, Protein: 14.63 g, Net Carbs: 11.67 g

64. Prosciutto and Mozzarella Bomb

Preparation Time: 15 minutes
Cooking Time: 10 minutes
Servings: 4
Ingredients:

- 4 oz. sliced prosciutto
- 8 oz. mozzarella ball
- Olive oil

Directions:

1. Layer half of the prosciutto vertically. Lay the remaining slices horizontally across the first set of slices. Place mozzarella ball, upside down, onto the crisscrossed prosciutto slices.
2. Wrap the mozzarella ball with the prosciutto slices. Heat the olive oil in a skillet, crisp the prosciutto, then serve.

Nutrition:
Calories: 253, Fats: 19.35 g, Protein: 18 g, Net Carbs: 1.08 g

65. Summer Tuna Avocado Salad

Preparation Time: 15 minutes
Cooking Time: 0 minutes
Servings: 2
Ingredients:
- 1 can tuna flake
- 1 medium avocado
- 1 medium English cucumber
- ¼ cup cilantro
- 1 Tbsp. lemon juice
- 1 Tbsp. olive oil
- Pepper
- Salt

Directions:
1. Put the first 4 ingredients into a salad bowl. Sprinkle with lemon and olive oil. Serve.

Nutrition:
Calories 303, Fats: 22.6 g, Protein: 16.7 g, Net Carbs: 5.2 g

66. Mushrooms & Goat Cheese Salad

Preparation Time: 15 minutes
Cooking Time: 10 minutes
Servings: 1
Ingredients:
- 1 Tbsp. butter
- 2 oz. cremini mushrooms
- Pepper
- Salt
- 4 oz. spring mix
- 1 oz. cooked bacon
- 1 oz. goat cheese
- 1 Tbsp. olive oil
- 1 Tbsp. balsamic vinegar

Directions:
1. Sautee the mushrooms, put pepper and salt.
2. Place the salad greens in a bowl. Top with goat cheese and crumbled bacon.
3. Mix these in the salad once the mushrooms are done.
4. Whisk the olive oil in a small bowl and balsamic vinegar. Put the salad on top and serve.

Nutrition:
Calories: 243, Fat: 21 g, Saturated Fat: 4 g, Carbs: 8 g, Fiber: 1 g

67. Keto Bacon Sushi

Preparation Time: 15 minutes
Cooking Time: 13 minutes
Servings: 4
Ingredients:
- 6 slices bacon
- 1 avocado
- 2 Persian cucumbers
- 2 medium carrots
- 4 oz. cream cheese

Directions:

Heat oven to 400°F. Line a baking sheet. Place bacon halves in an even layer and bake for 11 to 13 minutes.

Meanwhile, slice cucumbers, avocado, and carrots into parts roughly the width of the bacon.

Spread an even layer of cream cheese in the cooled-down bacon. Divide vegetables evenly and place them on one end. Roll up vegetables tightly. Garnish and serve.

Nutrition:

Carbohydrates: 11 g, Protein: 28 g, Fat: 30 g

68. Cole Slaw Keto Wrap

Preparation Time: 15 minutes
Cooking Time: 0 minutes
Servings: 2
Ingredients:
- 1/4 cup Red Cabbage
- 1/8 cup Green Onions
- 1/2 cup Mayo
- 2 tsp. Apple Cider Vinegar
- 25 tsp. Salt
- 16 pcs. Collard Green
- 1 lb. Ground Meat, cooked
- 1/4 cup Alfalfa Sprouts
- Toothpicks

Directions:
1. Mix slaw items with a spoon in a large-sized bowl.
2. Place a collard green on a plate and scoop a Tbsp. of coleslaw on the edge of the leaf. Top it with a scoop of meat and sprouts. Roll and tuck the sides.
3. Insert the toothpicks. Serve.

Nutrition:
Calories: 409, Fat: 42 g, Protein: 2 g, Net Carbs: 4 g, Fiber: 2 g,

69. Keto Chicken Club Lettuce Wrap

Preparation Time: 15 minutes
Cooking Time: 15 minutes
Servings: 1
Ingredients:
- 1 head iceberg lettuce
- 1 Tbsp. mayonnaise
- 6 slices of organic chicken
- 1 slice of Bacon
- 1 small tomato

Directions:
1. Layer 6-8 large leaves of lettuce in the center of the parchment paper, around 9-10 inches.
2. Spread the mayo in the center and lay with chicken, bacon, and tomato.
3. Roll the wrap halfway through, then roll tuck in the ends of the wrap.
4. Cut it in half. Serve.

Nutrition:
Calories: 837, Fat: 78 g, Protein: 28 g, Net Carbs: 4 g, Fiber: 2 g

70. Keto Broccoli Salad

Preparation Time: 10 minutes
Cooking Time: 0 minutes
Servings: 4-6
Ingredients:
For salad:
- 2 broccoli
- 2 red cabbage
- 1/2 cup sliced almonds
- 1 green onion
- 1/8 cup raisins

For the orange almond dressing
- 1/2 cup orange juice
- 1/4 cup almond butter
- 2 Tbsp. coconut aminos
- 1 shallot
- Salt

Directions:
1. Pulse the salt, shallot, amino, nut butter, and orange juice using a blender.
2. Combine other ingredients in a bowl. Toss it with dressing and serve.

Nutrition:
Calories: 1022, Fat: 94 g, Protein: 22 g, Net Carbs: 13 g, Fiber: 0 g

71. Keto Sheet Pan Chicken and Rainbow Veggies

Preparation Time: 15 minutes
Cooking Time: 25 minutes
Servings: 4
Ingredients:
- Nonstick spray
- 1 lb. Chicken Breasts
- 1 Tbsp. Sesame Oil
- 2 Tbsp. Soy Sauce
- 2 Tbsp. Honey
- 2 Red Pepper
- 2 Yellow Pepper
- 3 Carrots
- ½ Broccoli
- 2 Red Onions
- 2 Tbsp. EVOO
- Pepper & salt
- 1/4 cup Parsley

Directions:
1. Grease the baking sheet, Heat the oven to a temperature of 400°F.
2. Put the chicken in the middle of the sheet. Separately, combine the oil and the soy sauce. Brush over the chicken.
3. Separate veggies across the plate. Sprinkle with oil and then toss. Put pepper & salt.
4. Set tray into the oven and cook for 25 minutes. Garnish using parsley. Serve.

Nutrition:
Calories: 437, Fat: 30 g, Protein: 30 g, Net Carbs: 9 g, Fiber: 0 g

72. Skinny Bang-Bang Zucchini Noodles

Preparation Time: 15 minutes
Cooking Time: 15 minutes
Servings: 4
Ingredients:
For the noodles:

- 4 medium zucchinis spiraled
- 1 Tbsp. olive oil

For the sauce:

- 0.25 cup + 2 Tbsp. Plain Greek Yogurt
- 0.25 cup + 2 Tbsp. Mayo
- 0.25 cup + 2 Tbsp. Thai Sweet Chili Sauce
- 1 tsp. Honey
- 1 tsp. Sriracha
- 2 tsp. Lime Juice

Directions:

1. Pour the oil into a large skillet at medium temperature. Stir in the spiraled zucchini noodles. Cook.
2. Remove, then drain, and let it rest 10 minutes. Combine sauce items into a bowl.
3. Mix in the noodles to the sauce. Serve.

Nutrition:
Calories: 161, Fat: 1 g, Protein: 9 g, Net carbs: 18 g, Fiber: 0 g

73. Keto Caesar Salad

Preparation Time: 15 minutes
Cooking Time: 0 minutes
Servings: 4
Ingredients:
- 2 cups Mayonnaise
- 3 Tbsp. Apple Cider Vinegar
- 1 tsp. Dijon Mustard
- 4 Anchovy Fillets
- 24 Romaine Heart Leaves
- 4 oz Pork Rinds

Directions:
1. Process the mayo with ACV, mustard, and anchovies into a blender. Prepare romaine leaves and pour the dressing. Top with pork rinds and serve.

Nutrition:
Calories: 993, Fat: 86 g, Protein: 47 g, Net Carbs: 4 g, Fiber: 3 g

74. Keto Buffalo Chicken Empanadas

Preparation Time: 20 minutes
Cooking Time: 30 minutes
Servings: 6
Ingredients:
For the empanada dough:
- 1 ½ cups mozzarella cheese
- 3 oz. cream cheese
- 1 whisked egg
- 2 cups almond flour

For the buffalo chicken filling:
- 2 cups shredded chicken
- 2 Tbsp. Butter
- 0.33 cup Hot Sauce

Directions:
1. Heat oven, 425°F.
2. Microwave the cheese & cream cheese for 1 minute. Stir the flour and egg into the dish.
3. With another bowl, combine the chicken with sauce and set aside.
4. Cover a flat surface with plastic wrap and sprinkle with almond flour.
5. Grease a rolling pin, press the dough flat.
6. Make the circle shapes out of this dough with a lid.
7. Portion out spoonful of filling into these dough circles.
8. Fold the other half over to close up into half-moon shapes.
9. Bake for 9 minutes. Serve.

Nutrition:
Calories: 1217, Fat: 96 g, Protein: 74 g, Net Carbs: 20 g, Fiber: 0 g

75. Pepperoni and Cheddar Stromboli

Preparation Time: 15 minutes
Cooking Time: 20 minutes
Servings: 3
Ingredients:
- 2 cups Mozzarella Cheese
- 0.25 cup Almond Flour
- 3 Tbsp. Coconut Flour
- 1 tsp. Italian Seasoning
- 1 Egg
- 6 oz. Deli Ham
- 2 oz. Pepperoni
- 4 oz. Cheddar Cheese
- 1 Tbsp. Butter
- 6 cups Salad Greens

Directions:
1. Heat the oven, 400°F.
2. Melt the mozzarella. Mix flours and Italian seasoning in a separate bowl.
3. Dump in the melty cheese and mix with pepper and salt.
4. Stir in the egg and process the dough. Pour it onto that prepared baking tray.
5. Roll out the dough. Cut slits that mark out 4 equal rectangles.
6. Put the ham and cheese, then brush with butter and close up.
7. Bake for 17 minutes. Slice and serve.

Nutrition:
Calories: 240, Fat: 13 g, Protein: 11 g, Net carbs: 20 g, Fiber: 0 g

76. Tuna Casserole

Preparation Time: 15 minutes
Cooking Time: 10 minutes
Servings: 4
Ingredients:
- 16 oz. Tuna in oil
- 2 Tbsp. Butter
- Salt
- Black pepper
- 1 tsp. Chili powder
- 6 stalks Celery
- 1 Green bell pepper
- 1 Yellow onion,
- 4 oz. Parmesan cheese, grated
- 1 cup Mayonnaise

Directions:
1. Heat oven to 400°F.
2. Fry onion, bell pepper, and celery chops in the melted butter for 5 minutes.
3. Mix with chili powder, parmesan cheese, tuna, and mayonnaise.
4. Grease a baking pan. Add the tuna mixture into the fried vegetables.
5. Bake within twenty minutes. Serve.

Nutrition:
Calories 953, Fat: 83 g, Protein: 43 g, Net Carbs: 5 g,

77. Brussels Sprout and Hamburger Gratin

Preparation Time: 15 minutes
Cooking Time: 20 minutes
Servings: 4
Ingredients:

- 1 lb. Ground beef
- 8 oz. Bacon
- 15 oz. Brussel sprouts
- Salt
- Black pepper
- 1 ½ tsp. Thyme
- 1 cup Cheddar cheese
- 1 Tbsp. Italian seasoning
- 4 Tbsp. Sour cream
- 2 Tbsp. Butter

Directions:

1. Heat oven to 425°F.
2. Fry bacon and Brussel sprouts in butter for five minutes.
3. Stir in the sour cream and put it into a greased baking pan.
4. Cook the ground beef and put salt and pepper, then add this mix to the baking pan.
5. Top with the herbs and the shredded cheese. Bake for 20 minutes. Serve.

Nutrition:
Calories: 770, Fat: 62 g, Protein: 42 g, Net Carbs: 8 g

78. Carpaccio

Preparation Time: 15 minutes
Cooking Time: 5 minutes
Servings: 4
Ingredients:
- 100 g smoked prime rib
- 30 g arugula
- 20 g Parmesan cheese
- 10 g pine nuts
- 7 g butter
- 3 Tbsp. olive oil with orange
- 1 Tbsp. lemon juice
- Pepper
- Salt

Directions:
1. Arrange the meat slices on a plate. Place the arugula on top of the meat.
2. Spread Parmesan cheese over the arugula.
3. Put the butter in a frying pan. Add the pine nuts, bake for a few minutes over medium heat and then sprinkle them over the carpaccio.
4. For the vinaigrette, mix the lemon juice into the olive oil, put pepper and salt, and drizzle over the carpaccio. Serve.

Nutrition:
Calories: 350, Fat: 24 g, Protein: 31 g, Carbohydrates: 2 g, Fiber: 1 g

79. Keto Croque Monsieur

Preparation Time: 15 minutes
Cooking Time: 7 minutes
Servings: 4
Ingredients:
- 2 eggs
- 25 grams grated cheese
- 25 grams ham
- 40 ml cream
- 40 ml mascarpone
- 30 grams butter
- Pepper
- Salt
- Basil leaves

Directions:
1. Beat eggs in a bowl, put salt and pepper.
2. Add the cream, mascarpone, and grated cheese and mix.
3. Melt the butter over medium heat. Adjust the heat to low.
4. Add half of the omelet mixture to the frying pan and then place a slice of ham. Put the rest of the omelet mixture over the ham. Fry for 2-3 minutes over low heat.
5. Then, put the omelet back in the frying pan to fry for another 1-2 minutes.
6. Garnish with a few basil leaves. Serve.

Nutrition:
Calories: 350, Fat: 24 g, Protein: 31 g, Carbohydrates: 2 g, Fiber: 1 g

80. Keto Wraps with Cream Cheese and Salmon

Preparation Time: 15 minutes
Cooking Time: 10 minutes
Servings: 4
Ingredients:
- 80 g cream cheese
- 1 Tbsp. dill
- 30 g smoked salmon
- 1 egg
- 15 grams butter
- Pinch cayenne pepper
- Pepper
- Salt

Directions:
1. Beat the egg well in a bowl.
2. Dissolve the butter over medium heat in a small frying pan. Put half of the beaten egg into the pan.
3. Carefully loosen the egg on the edges with a silicone spatula and turn the wafer-thin omelet, about 45 seconds each side. Remove.
4. Cut the dill into small pieces and put them in a bowl.
5. Add the cream cheese and the salmon, cut into small pieces. Mix.
6. Put a cayenne pepper and mix. Put salt and pepper.
7. Spread a layer on the wrap and roll it up. Cut the wrap in half and serve.

Nutrition:
Calories: 479, Fats: 45 g, Protein: 16 g, Net carbohydrates: 4 g

81. Savory Keto Broccoli Cheese Muffins

Preparation Time: 15 minutes
Cooking Time: 10 minutes
Servings: 4
Ingredients:

- 4 eggs
- 75 g Parmesan cheese
- 125 g young cheese
- 125 g mozzarella
- 75 g broccoli
- 1 tsp. baking powder
- 0.25 tsp. garlic powder
- 0.25 tsp. mustard

Directions:

1. Heat-up oven to 160°C.
2. Boil water into a saucepan, put the broccoli pieces for 1 minute. Drain.
3. Grate the parmesan cheese and the young cheese. Cut the mozzarella into small pieces.
4. Beat the eggs, put the broccoli, cheese, and mustard.
5. Then add the garlic powder and baking powder and mix.
6. Fill a silicone muffin tray with the broccoli-cheese egg batter and bake for 10 minutes. Serve.

Nutrition:
Calories: 349, Fats: 25 g, Protein: 28 g, Carbohydrates: 3 g, Fiber: 1 g

CHAPTER 11:

DINNER RECIPES

82. Mexican Shredded Beef

Preparation Time: 10 minutes
Cooking Time: 7 hours and 15 minutes
Servings: 8
Ingredients:
- 3 1/2 lb. Beef short ribs, grass-fed
- 2 Tbsp. Minced garlic - 2 tsp. Ground turmeric
- 1 tsp. Salt - 1/2 tsp. Ground black pepper
- 2 tsp. Ground cumin
- 2 tsp. Ground coriander
- 1 tsp. Chipotle powder
- 1/2 cup Water
- 1 cup Cilantro stems, chopped

Directions:
1. Place salt in a small bowl, add black pepper, cumin, coriander, chipotle powder, and stir until mixed.
2. Place ribs into the slow cooker, sprinkle well with the prepared spice mixture, and then top with minced garlic and cilantro stems.
3. Switch on the slow cooker, pour in water, then cover with the lid and cook for 6 to 7 hours over low heat setting or until tender.
4. Then, pour the sauce into a small saucepan and cook for 10 to 15 minutes or until reduced by half. Return the sauce into the slow cooker, pull apart the meat and toss until well mixed.
5. Portion out beef into eight glass meal prep containers, then cover with a lid and store in the refrigerator for up to 5 days or freeze for up to 2 months.
6. When ready to serve, reheat the beef in its glass container in the microwave for 1 to 2 minutes or until hot.

Nutrition:
Calories: 656; Fat: 48.5 g; Protein: 50.2 g; Net Carbs: 1 g; Fiber: 0.4 g

83. Beef Stew

Preparation Time: 5 minutes
Cooking Time: 8 hours and 5 minutes
Servings: 4
Ingredients:

- 3 1/2 lb. Beef, grass-fed, diced
- 3 Stalks celery, chopped
- 1 Leek, white part only
- 15 oz. Diced tomatoes
- ¾ cup Spinach leaves, fresh
- 3 Carrots, chopped into large rounds
- 1 Tbsp. Chopped ginger
- ½ Tbsp. Minced garlic - 1 ½ tsp. Salt
- ¾ tsp. Ground black pepper
- 2 tsp. Dried rosemary
- 2 tsp. Dried thyme - 2 tsp. Dried oregano
- 2 Tbsp. Apple cider vinegar
- 2 Tbsp. Avocado oil
- 1 1/2 cups Beef broth, grass-fed

Directions:

1. Take a frying pan, place it over medium heat, add oil and when hot, add beef and cook for 3 to 5 minutes or until light brown.
2. Transfer beef into a slow cooker, add remaining ingredients, except for spinach, and stir until mixed.
3. Switch on the slow cooker, shut it with a lid and cook for 5 to 8 hours at a low heat setting until thoroughly cooked.
4. When beef cooking is about to finish, place spinach in a heatproof bowl, cover with plastic wrap, and microwave for 2 minutes until steamed.
5. When beef is cooked, taste to adjust seasoning, add spinach and stir until just mixed and let cool. Divide beef evenly between four glass containers, then cover with lid and store in the refrigerator for up to 5 days or freeze for up to 2 months.
6. When ready to serve, thaw the stew at room temperature and then reheat the beef stew in its glass container in the microwave for 2 to 3 minutes or until hot.
7. Serve the stew with cauliflower rice.

Nutrition:
Calories: 553; Fat: 36.9 g; Protein: 175 g; Net Carbs: 4.8 g; Fiber: 1.6 g

84. Coconut Shrimp

Preparation Time: 10 minutes
Cooking Time: 12 minutes
Servings: 4
Ingredients:

- 1 lb. Medium-sized shrimp, wild-caught, peeled, deveined
- 3 Tbsp. Coconut flour
- 1/4 tsp. Garlic powder
- 3 Eggs, Pastured, beaten
- 1 3/4 cup Coconut flakes, unsweetened
- 1/8 tsp. Ground black pepper
- 1/4 tsp. Smoked paprika
- 1/4 tsp. Sea salt

Directions:

1. Set the oven to 400°F and let preheat.
2. Meanwhile, crack eggs in a bowl and whisk until beaten, place coconut flakes in another dish, then place coconut flour in another dish; add salt, black pepper, garlic powder, and paprika and stir until mixed.
3. Working on one piece at a time, dredge a shrimp into the coconut flour mix, then dip into egg, and dredge with coconut flake until evenly coated.
4. Take a non-stick wire rack, line it with a baking sheet, then spray with oil and place coated shrimps on it in a single layer.
5. Place the wire rack containing shrimps into the oven, bake for 4 minutes, then flip the shrimps and continue baking for 5 to 6 minutes or until thoroughly cooked and firm.
6. Then, switch on the broiler and bake the shrimps for 2 minutes or until lightly golden.
7. When done, let shrimps cooled, place them on a baking sheet in a single layer, then cover the shrimps with a parchment sheet, layer with remaining shrimps and freeze until hard.
8. Then, transfer shrimps into a freezer bag and store them in the freezer for up to 3 months.
9. When ready to serve, reheat the shrimps at 350°F for 2 to 3 minutes until hot.

Nutrition:
Calories: 443; Fat: 30 g; Protein: 31 g; Net Carbs: 5 g; Fiber: 7 g

85. Sausage Stuffed Zucchini Boats

Preparation Time: 10 minutes
Cooking Time: 30 minutes
Servings: 4
Ingredients:

- 4 Medium zucchini - 1 lb. Ground Italian pork sausage, pastured
- 1 ½ tsp. Sea salt
- 1/3 cup Medium white onion, peeled, diced
- 1 Tbsp. Minced garlic - 1 tsp. Italian seasoning
- 14.5 oz. Diced tomatoes
- 1/3 cup Grated parmesan cheese, full-fat
- 2 Tbsp. Avocado oil, divided
- 1 cup Mozzarella cheese, full-fat, shredded

Directions:

1. Set the oven to 400°F and let preheat.
2. Meanwhile, cut each zucchini in half, lengthwise, then make a well in the center by scooping out the centers by using a spoon.
3. Take a baking sheet, line it with a parchment sheet, place zucchini halves on it, cut side up, drizzle with 1 Tbsp. oil, and season with salt.
4. Place the baking sheet into the oven and bake for 15 to 20 minutes or until soft.
5. Meanwhile, take a large skillet pan, place it over medium-high heat, add remaining oil and when hot, add onions and cook for 10 minutes until nicely brown. Add sausage, stir well and cook for 5 minutes or until brown.
6. Then, move sausage to one side of the pan, add garlic to the other side, cook for 1 minute or until fragrant, and then mix into the sausage.
7. Remove the pan from the heat, season sausage with Italian seasoning, add tomatoes and parmesan cheese, stir well and taste to adjust seasoning.
8. When zucchini halves are roasted, pat dry with paper towels, then stuff with sausage mixture.
9. Top stuffed zucchini with mozzarella cheese and bake for 5 to 10 minutes or until cheese melts, and the top is nicely golden brown.
10. Let zucchini boats cool down, then wrap each zucchini boat with aluminum foil and freeze in the freezer.
11. When ready to serve, thaw the zucchini boat and reheat at 350°F for 3 to 4 minutes until hot.

Nutrition:

Calories: 582; Fat: 44 g; Protein: 29 g; Net Carbs: 11 g; Fiber: 3 g

86. Balsamic Steaks

Preparation Time: 3 hours and 10 minutes
Cooking Time: 10 minutes
Servings: 4
Ingredients:
- 4 Sirloin steaks, each about 8 oz., grass-fed
- 1 Tbsp. Butter, unsalted

For the marinade:
- 1/2 tsp. Garlic powder
- 1/4 cup Coconut aminos
- 1/2 tsp. Ground black pepper
- 1/4 cup Avocado oil
- 2 Tbsp. Balsamic vinegar
- 1 tsp. Italian seasoning
- 1 tsp. Sea salt

Directions:
1. Place all the ingredients for the marinade in a bowl, whisk until well combined, and then pour the mixture into a large freezer bag.
2. Add steaks into the bag, seal the bag, then turn it upside side or until steaks are coated with the marinade and place it in the refrigerator for 3 hours.
3. When ready to cook, set the oven to 400°F and let preheat.
4. In the meantime, take out steaks from the refrigerator and let them rest at room temperature.
5. Then, take a large skillet pan, place it over medium heat, add butter and when it melts, add steaks in a single layer and cook for 2 minutes per side or until seared.
6. Transfer the pan into the oven and bake the stakes for 3 to 6 minutes or until cooked to desired doneness, such as 3 minutes or 120°F for medium-rare doneness, 4 minutes or 140°F for medium doneness, 5 minutes or 150°F for medium-well doneness, and 6 minutes or 160°F for a well-done steak.
7. Transfer the steaks to a plate, let them rest for 5 minutes, and cut into slices.
8. Then transfer steaks into a freezer bag and store in the freezer for up to 3 months.
9. When ready to serve, reheat the steak slices into a hot skillet pan until warm through.

Nutrition:
Calories: 450; Fat: 24 g; Protein: 49 g; Net Carbs: 5 g; Fiber: 0 g

87. Chicken Pan with Veggies and Pesto

Preparation Time: 10 minutes
Cooking Time: 20 minutes
Servings: 4
Ingredients:
- 2 Tbsp. olive oil
- 1 lb. chicken thighs, boneless, skinless, sliced into strips
- ¾ cup oil-packed sun-dried tomatoes, chopped
- 1 lb. asparagus ends
- ¼ cup basil pesto
- 1 cup cherry tomatoes, red and yellow, halved
- Salt, to taste

Directions:
1. Heat olive oil in a frying pan over medium-high heat.
2. Put salt on the chicken slices and put them into a skillet, add the sun-dried tomatoes and fry for 5-10 minutes. Remove the chicken slices and season with salt. Add asparagus to the skillet. Cook for additional 5-10 minutes.
3. Place the chicken back in the skillet, pour in the pesto, and whisk. Fry for 1-2 minutes. Remove from the heat. Add the halved cherry tomatoes and pesto. Stir well and serve.

Nutrition:
Calories: 423, Fat: 32 g, Protein: 2 g, Carbohydrates: 12 g

88. Cabbage Soup with Beef

Preparation Time: 15 minutes
Cooking Time: 20 minutes
Servings: 4
Ingredients:

- 2 Tbsp. olive oil
- 1 medium onion, chopped
- 1 lb. fillet steak, cut into pieces
- ½ stalk celery, chopped
- 1 carrot, peeled and diced
- ½ head small green cabbage, cut into pieces
- 2 cloves garlic, minced
- 4 cups beef broth
- 2 Tbsp. fresh parsley, chopped
- 1 tsp. garlic powder
- Salt and black pepper, to taste

Directions:

1. Heat oil in a pot (use medium heat). Add the beef and cook until it is browned. Put the onion into the pot and boil for 3-4 minutes.
2. Add the celery and carrot. Stir well and cook for about 3-4 minutes. Add the cabbage and boil until it starts softening. Add garlic and simmer for about 1 minute.
3. Pour the broth into the pot. Add the parsley and garlic powder. Mix thoroughly and reduce heat to medium-low.
4. Cook for 10-15 minutes.

Nutrition:
Calories: 177, Fat: 11 g, Protein: 12 g, Carbohydrates: 4 g

89. Cauliflower Rice Soup with Chicken

Preparation Time: 10 minutes
Cooking Time: 1 hour
Servings: 5
Ingredients:

- 2½ lb. chicken breasts, boneless and skinless
- 8 Tbsp. butter
- ¼ cup celery, chopped
- ½ cup onion, chopped
- 4 cloves garlic, minced
- 2 ½ oz. packages steamed cauliflower rice
- ½ cup carrot, grated
- ¾ tsp. rosemary
- 1 tsp. salt
- ¾ tsp. pepper
- 4¾ cup chicken broth

Directions:

1. Put shredded chicken breasts into a saucepan and pour in the chicken broth. Add salt and pepper. Cook for 1 hour.
2. In another pot, melt the butter. Add the onion, garlic, and celery. Sauté until the mix is translucent. Add the cauliflower rice, rosemary, and carrot. Mix and cook for 7 minutes.
3. Add the chicken breasts and broth to the cauliflower mix. Put the lid on and simmer for 15 minutes.

Nutrition:

Calories: 415, Fat: 30 g, Protein: 27 g, Carbohydrates: 6 g

90. Quick Pumpkin Soup

Preparation Time: 10 minutes
Cooking Time: 20 minutes
Servings: 4-6
Ingredients:
- 1 cup coconut milk
- 2 cups chicken broth
- 6 cups baked pumpkin
- 1 tsp. garlic powder
- 1 tsp. ground cinnamon
- 1 tsp. dried ginger
- 1 tsp. nutmeg
- 1 tsp. paprika
- Salt and pepper, to taste
- Sour cream or coconut yogurt, for topping
- Pumpkin seeds, toasted, for topping

Directions:
1. Combine the coconut milk, broth, baked pumpkin, and spices in a soup pan (use medium heat). Stir occasionally and simmer for 15 minutes.
2. With an immersion blender, blend the soup mix for 1 minute.
3. Top with sour cream or coconut yogurt and pumpkin seeds.

Nutrition:
Calories: 123, Fat: 9.8 g, Protein: 3.1 g, Carbohydrates: 8.1 g

91. Fresh Avocado Soup

Preparation Time: 5 minutes
Cooking Time: 10 minutes
Servings: 2
Ingredients:
- 1 ripe avocado
- 2 romaine lettuce leaves, washed and chopped
- 1 cup coconut milk, chilled
- 1 Tbsp. lime juice
- 20 fresh mint leaves
- Salt, to taste

Directions:
1. Mix all your ingredients thoroughly in a blender.
2. Chill in the fridge for 5-10 minutes.

Nutrition:
Calories: 280, Fat: 26 g, Protein: 4 g, Carbohydrates: 12 g

92. Green Chicken Curry

Preparation Time: 15 minutes
Cooking Time: 30 minutes
Servings: 4
Ingredients:
- 1 lb. grass-fed chicken breasts
- 1 Tbsp. olive oil
- 2 Tbsp. green curry paste
- 1 cup unsweetened coconut milk
- 1 cup chicken broth
- 1 cup asparagus spears
- 1 cup green beans
- Salt
- Ground black pepper
- ¼ cup basil leaves

Directions:
1. Sauté the curry paste for 1–2 minutes. Add the chicken and cook for 8–10 minutes.
2. Add coconut milk and broth, boil. Cook again in low for 8–10 minutes.
3. Add the asparagus, green beans, salt and black pepper, and cook for 4–5 minutes.
4. Serve.

Nutrition:
Calories: 294, Total Fat: 16.2 g, Protein: 28.6 g, Net Carbs: 4.3 g

93. Creamy Pork Stew

Preparation Time: 15 minutes
Cooking Time: 1 hour 35 minutes
Servings: 8
Ingredients:
- 3 Tbsp. unsalted butter
- 2½ lb. boneless pork ribs
- 1 yellow onion
- 4 garlic cloves
- 1½ cups chicken broth
- 2 cans sugar-free diced tomatoes
- 2 tsp. dried oregano
- 1 tsp. ground cumin
- Salt
- 2 Tbsp. lime juice
- ½ cup sour cream

Directions:
1. Cook the pork, onions, and garlic for 4–5 minutes. Add the broth, tomatoes, oregano, cumin, and salt, and mix. Simmer to low. Combine in the sour cream and lime juice and remove. Serve.

Nutrition:
Calories: 304, Total Fat: 12.4 g, Protein: 39.5 g, Net Carbs: 4.7 g

94. Salmon & Shrimp Stew

Preparation Time: 20 minutes
Cooking Time: 25 minutes
Servings: 6
Ingredients:
- 2 Tbsp. coconut oil
- ½ cup onion
- 2 garlic cloves
- 1 Serrano pepper
- 1 tsp. smoked paprika
- 2 cups sliced tomatoes
- 4 cups chicken broth
- 1 lb. salmon fillets
- 1 lb. shrimp
- 2 Tbsp. lime juice
- Salt
- Ground black pepper
- 3 Tbsp. parsley

Directions:
1. Sauté the onion for 5–6 minutes. Add the garlic, Serrano pepper, and paprika. Add the tomatoes and broth, then boil. Simmer for 5 minutes. Add the salmon and simmer again for 3–4 minutes.
2. Put in the shrimp, then cook for 4–5 minutes. Mix in lemon juice, salt, and black pepper, and remove. Serve with parsley.

Nutrition:
Calories: 247, Fiber: 1.2 g, Sugar: 2.1 g, Protein: 32.7 g, Net Carbs: 3.9 g

95. Chicken Casserole

Preparation Time: 15 minutes
Cooking Time: 1 hour 10 minutes
Servings: 6
Ingredients:
Chicken Layer:
- 6 grass-fed chicken breasts
- Salt
- Ground black pepper

Bacon Layer:
- 5 bacon slices
- ¼ cup yellow onion
- ¼ cup jalapeño pepper
- ½ cup mayonnaise
- 1 package cream cheese
- ½ cup Parmesan cheese
- 1 cup cheddar cheese

Topping:
- 1 package pork skins
- ¼ cup butter
- ½ cup Parmesan cheese

Directions:
1. Heat the oven to 425°F.
2. Put the chicken breasts in the greased casserole, then put salt and black pepper.
3. Bake for 30–40 minutes.

For the bacon layer:
4. Cook the bacon for 8–10 minutes. Transfer.
5. Sauté onion for 4–5 minutes. Remove, stir in bacon, and remaining ingredients.
6. Remove the casserole dish, then put the bacon mixture.
7. Mix all topping ingredients. Place the topping over the bacon mixture. Bake for 15 minutes. Serve.

Nutrition:
Calories: 826, Total Fat: 62.9 g, Protein: 60.6 g, Net Carbs: 2.5 g

96. Creamy Chicken Bake

Preparation Time: 15 minutes
Cooking Time: 1 hour 10 minutes
Servings: 6
Ingredients:

- 5 Tbsp. unsalted butter
- 2 onions
- 3 garlic cloves
- 1 tsp. tarragon
- 8 oz. cream cheese
- 1 cup chicken broth
- 2 Tbsp. lemon juice
- ½ cup heavy cream
- 1½ tsp. Herbs de Provence
- Salt
- Ground black pepper
- 4 grass-fed chicken breasts

Directions:

1. Heat the oven to 350°F.
2. Cook the onion, garlic, and tarragon for 4–5 minutes. Transfer.
3. Cook the cream cheese, ½ cup of broth, and lemon juice for 3–4 minutes.
4. Stir in the cream, herbs de Provence, salt, and black pepper, remove.
5. Pour remaining broth and chicken breast plus the cream mixture. Bake for 45–60 minutes. Serve.

Nutrition:
Calories: 729, Total Fat: 52.8 g, Protein: 55.8 g, Net Carbs: 5.6 g, Sugar: 2 g

97. Beef & Veggie Casserole

Preparation Time: 20 minutes
Cooking Time: 55 minutes
Servings: 6
Ingredients:

- 3 Tbsp. butter
- 1 lb. grass-fed ground beef
- 1 yellow onion
- 2 garlic cloves
- 1 cup pumpkin
- 1 cup broccoli
- 2 cups cheddar cheese
- 1 Tbsp. Dijon mustard
- 6 organic eggs
- ½ cup heavy whipping cream
- Salt
- Ground black pepper

Directions:

1. Cook the beef for 8–10 minutes. Transfer.
2. Cook the onion and garlic for 10 minutes. Add the pumpkin and cook for 5–6 minutes.
3. Add the broccoli and cook for 3–4 minutes. Transfer to the cooked beef, combine.
4. Heat the oven to 350°F.
5. Put 2/3 of cheese and mustard in the beef mixture, combine.
6. In another mixing bowl, add cream, eggs, salt, and black pepper, and beat.
7. In a baking dish, place the beef mixture and top with egg mixture, plus the remaining cheese.
8. Bake for 25 minutes. Serve.

Nutrition:
Calories: 472, Total Fat: 34.6 g, Protein: 32.6 g, Net Carbs: 5.5 g, Sodium: 463 mg

98. Beef with Bell Peppers

Preparation Time: 15 minutes
Cooking Time: 10 minutes
Servings: 4

Ingredients:
- 1 Tbsp. olive oil
- 1 lb. grass-fed flank steak
- 1 red bell pepper
- 1 green bell pepper
- 1 Tbsp. ginger
- 3 Tbsp. low-sodium soy sauce
- 1½ Tbsp. balsamic vinegar
- 2 tsp. Sriracha

Directions:
1. Sear the steak slices for 2 minutes. Cook bell peppers for 2–3 minutes.
2. Transfer the beef mixture. Boil the remaining ingredients for 1 minute. Add the beef mixture and cook for 1–2 minutes. Serve.

Nutrition:
Calories: 274, Total Fat: 13.1 g, Protein: 32.9 g, Net Carbs: 3.8 g

99. Braised Lamb shanks

Preparation Time: 15 minutes
Cooking Time: 2 hours 35 minutes
Servings: 4
Ingredients:
- 4 grass-fed lamb shanks
- 2 Tbsp. butter
- Salt
- Ground black pepper
- 6 garlic cloves
- 6 rosemary sprigs
- 1 cup chicken broth

Directions:
1. Heat the oven to 450°F.
2. Coat the shanks with butter and put salt and pepper. Roast for 20 minutes.
3. Remove, then reduce to 325°F.
4. Place the garlic cloves and rosemary over and around the lamb.
5. Roast for 2 hours. Put the broth into a roasting pan.
6. Increase to 400°F. Roast for 15 minutes more. Serve.

Nutrition:
Calories: 1093, Total Fat: 44.2 g, Protein: 161.4 g, Net Carbs: 2 g

100. Shrimp & Bell Pepper Stir-Fry

Preparation Time: 20 minutes
Cooking Time: 10 minutes
Servings: 6
Ingredients:

- ½ cup low-sodium soy sauce
- 2 Tbsp. balsamic vinegar
- 2 Tbsp. Erythritol
- 1 Tbsp. arrowroot starch
- 1 Tbsp. ginger
- ½ tsp. red pepper flakes
- 3 Tbsp. olive oil
- ½ red bell pepper
- ½ yellow bell pepper
- ½ green bell pepper
- 1 onion
- 1 red chili
- 1½ lb. shrimp
- 2 scallion greens

Directions:

1. Mix soy sauce, vinegar, erythritol, arrowroot starch, ginger, and red pepper flakes. Set aside.
2. Stir-fry the bell peppers, onion, and red chili for 1–2 minutes.
3. In the center of the wok, place the shrimp and cook for 1–2 minutes.
4. Stir the shrimp with bell pepper mixture and cook for 2 minutes.
5. Stir in the sauce and cook for 2–3 minutes.
6. Stir in the scallion greens and remove. Serve hot.

Nutrition:
Calories: 221, Total Fat: 9 g, Protein: 27.6 g, Net Carbs: 6.5 g

101. Veggies & Walnut Loaf

Preparation Time: 15 minutes
Cooking Time: 1 hour 10 minutes
Servings: 10
Ingredients:

- 1 Tbsp. olive oil
- 2 yellow onions
- 2 garlic cloves
- 1 tsp. dried rosemary
- 1 cup walnuts
- 2 carrots
- 1 celery stalk
- 1 green bell pepper
- 1 cup button mushrooms
- 5 organic eggs
- 1¼ cups almond flour
- Salt
- Ground black pepper

Directions:

1. Heat the oven to 350°F. Sauté the onion for 4–5 minutes.
2. Add the garlic and rosemary and sauté for 1 minute.
3. Add the walnuts and vegetables for 3–4 minutes. Put aside.
4. Beat the eggs, flour, sea salt, and black pepper.
5. Mix the egg mixture with vegetable mixture.
6. Bake for 50–60 minutes. Serve.

Nutrition:
Calories: 242, Total Fat: 19.5 g, Protein: 5.9 g, Net Carbs: 4.6 g

102. Keto Sloppy Joes

Preparation Time: 15 minutes
Cooking Time: 1 hour 10 minutes
Servings: 3
Ingredients:
- 1 ¼ cup almond flour
- 5 Tbsp. ground psyllium husk powder
- 1 tsp. sea salt
- 2 tsp. baking powder
- 2 tsp. cider vinegar
- 1 ¼ cups boiling water
- 3 egg whites
- 2 Tbsp. olive oil
- 1 ½ lb. ground beef
- 1 yellow onion
- 4 garlic cloves
- 14 oz. crushed tomatoes
- 1 Tbsp. chili powder
- 1 Tbsp. Dijon powder
- 1 Tbsp. red wine vinegar
- 4 Tbsp. tomato paste
- 2 tsp. salt
- ¼ tsp. ground black pepper
- ½ cup mayonnaise
- 6 oz. cheese

Directions:
1. Heat the oven to 350°F and then mix all the dry ingredients.
2. Add some vinegar, egg whites, and boiled water. Whisk for 30 seconds.
3. Form the dough into 5 or 8 pieces of bread. Cook for 55 minutes.
4. Cook the onion and garlic. Add the ground beef and cook. Put the other ingredients and cook. Simmer for 10 minutes in low. Serve.

Nutrition:
Calories: 215, Fat: 10 g, Protein: 30 g, Carbs: 19 g

103. Low Carb Crack Slaw Egg Roll in a Bowl Recipe

Preparation Time: 15 minutes
Cooking Time: 20 minutes
Servings: 2
Ingredients:

- 1 lb. ground beef
- 4 cups shredded coleslaw mix
- 1 Tbsp. avocado oil
- 1 tsp. Sea salt
- ¼ tsp. black pepper
- 4 cloves garlic
- 3 Tbsp. ginger
- ¼ cup coconut amines
- 2 tsp. toasted sesame oil
- ¼ cup green onions

Directions:

1. Heat avocado oil in a large pan, put in the garlic, and cook.
2. Add the ground beef and cook for 10 minutes, put salt and black pepper.
3. Lower the heat and add the coleslaw mix and the coconut amines. Stir to cook for 5 minutes.
4. Remove and put in the green onions and the toasted sesame oil. Serve.

Nutrition:

Calories: 116, Carbs: 2 g, Fat: 13 g, Protein: 8 g

104. Low Carb Beef Stir Fry

Preparation Time: 15 minutes
Cooking Time: 20 minutes
Servings: 4
Ingredients:
- ½ cup zucchini
- ¼ cup organic broccoli florets
- 1 baby book Choy
- 2 Tbsp. avocado oil
- 2 tsp. coconut amines
- 1/8 cup Ghee
- 1 small ginger
- 8 oz. skirt steak

Directions:
1. Sear the steak on high heat. Adjust to medium and put in the broccoli, ginger, ghee, and coconut amines. Add in the book Choy and cook for another minute.
2. Put the zucchini into the mix and cook. Serve.

Nutrition:
Calories: 275, Fat: 5 g, Protein: 40 g, Carbs: 12 g

105. One Pan Pesto Chicken and Veggies

Preparation Time: 15 minutes
Cooking Time: 25 minutes
Servings: 4
Ingredients:
- 2 Tbsp. olive oil
- 1 cup cherry diced tomatoes
- ¼ cup basil pesto
- 1/3 cup sun-dried tomatoes
- 1 lb. chicken thigh
- 1 lb. asparagus

Directions:
1. Heat a large skillet. Put two Tbsp. of olive oil and sliced chicken on medium heat. Put salt and add ½ cup of sun-dried tomatoes. Cook. Transfer the chicken and tomatoes.
2. Put the asparagus in the skillet and pour it into the pesto. Put the remaining sun-dried tomatoes. Cook for 5 to 10 minutes. Transfer.
3. Turn the chicken back in the skillet and pour it into pesto. Stir for 2 minutes. Serve with the asparagus.

Nutrition:
Calories: 340, Fat: 24 g, Protein: 23 g, Carbs: 9 g

106. Crispy Peanut Tofu and Cauliflower Rice Stir-Fry

Preparation Time: 15 minutes
Cooking Time: 1 hour
Servings: 4
Ingredients:

- 12 oz. tofu
- 1 Tbsp. toasted sesame oil
- 2 cloves minced garlic
- 1 cauliflower head

Sauce:

- 1 ½ Tbsp. Toasted sesame oil
- ½ tsp. chili garlic sauce
- 2 ½ Tbsp. peanut butter
- ¼ cup low sodium soy sauce
- ½ cup light brown sugar

Directions:

1. Heat the oven to 400°F. Cube the tofu.
2. Bake for 25 minutes and cool.
3. Combine the sauce ingredients. Put the tofu in the sauce and stir. Leave for 15 minutes.
4. Cook the veggies on a bit of sesame oil and soy sauce. Set it aside.
5. Grab the tofu and put it on the pan. Stir, then set aside.
6. Steam the cauliflower rice for 5 to 8 minutes. Add some sauce and stir.
7. Add up the ingredients. Put the cauliflower rice with the veggies and tofu. Serve.

Nutrition:
Calories: 524, Fat: 34 g, Protein: 25 g, Carbs: 39 g

107. Simple Keto Fried Chicken

Preparation Time: 15 minutes
Cooking Time: 45 minutes
Servings: 4
Ingredients:
- 4 boneless chicken thighs
- Frying oil
- 2 eggs
- 2 Tbsp. heavy whipping cream

Breading:
- 2/3 cup grated parmesan cheese
- 2/3 cup blanched almond flour
- 1 tsp. salt
- ½ tsp. black pepper
- ½ tsp. cayenne
- ½ tsp. paprika

Directions:
1. Beat the eggs and heavy cream. Separately, mix all the breading ingredients. Set aside.
2. Cut the chicken thigh into 3 even pieces.
3. Dip the chicken in the bread first before dipping it in the egg wash and then finally, dipping it in the breading again. Fry chicken for 5 minutes. Pat dry the chicken. Serve.

Nutrition:
Calories: 304, Fat: 15 g, Protein: 30 g, Carbs: 12 g

108. Keto Butter Chicken

Preparation Time: 15 minutes
Cooking Time: 20 minutes
Servings: 4
Ingredients:
- 1.5 lb. chicken breast
- 1 Tbsp. coconut oil
- 2 Tbsp. garam masala
- 3 tsp. grated ginger
- 3 tsp. garlic
- 4 oz. plain yogurt

Sauce:
- 2 Tbsp. butter
- 1 Tbsp. ground coriander
- ½ cup heavy cream
- ½ Tbsp. garam masala
- 2 tsp. ginger
- 2 tsp. minced garlic
- 2 tsp. cumin
- 1 tsp. chili powder
- 1 onion
- 14.5 oz. crushed tomatoes
- Salt

Directions:
1. Mix chicken pieces, 2 tbsps. of garam masala, 1 tsp. of minced garlic, and 1 tsp. of grated ginger. Stir and add the yogurt. Chill for 30 minutes.
2. For the sauce, blend the ginger, garlic, onion, tomatoes, and spices. Put aside.
3. Cook the chicken pieces. Once cooked, pour in the sauce, and simmer for 5 minutes. Serve.

Nutrition:
Calories: 367, Fat: 22 g, Protein: 36 g, Carbs: 7 g,

109. Keto Shrimp Scampi Recipe

Preparation Time: 15 minutes
Cooking Time: 25 minutes
Servings: 2
Ingredients:

- 2 summer squash
- 1 lb. shrimp
- 2 Tbsp. butter unsalted
- 2 Tbsp. lemon juice
- 2 Tbsp. parsley
- ¼ cup chicken broth
- 1/8 tsp. red chili flakes
- 1 clove garlic
- Salt
- Pepper

Directions:

1. Put salt in the squash noodles on top. Set aside for 30 minutes.
2. Pat dry. Fry the garlic. Add some chicken broth, red chili flakes, and lemon juice.
3. Once it boils, add the shrimp, and cook. Lower the heat.
4. Add salt and pepper, put the summer squash noodles and parsley into the mix. Serve.

Nutrition:
Calories: 366, Fat: 15 g, Protein: 49 g, Carbs: 7 g

110. Keto Lasagna

Preparation Time: 15 minutes
Cooking Time: 1 hour
Servings: 2
Ingredients:
- 8 oz. block cream cheese
- 3 eggs
- Kosher salt
- Ground black pepper
- 2 cups mozzarella
- ½ cup parmesan
- Pinch red pepper flakes
- Parsley

Sauce:
- ¾ cup marinara
- 1 Tbsp. tomato paste
- 1 lb. ground beef
- ½ cup parmesan
- 1.5 cup mozzarella
- 1 Tbsp. extra virgin olive oil
- 1 tsp. dried oregano
- 3 cloves garlic
- ½ cup onion - 16 oz. ricotta

Directions:
1. Heat the oven to 350°F.
2. Melt in the cream cheese, mozzarella, and parmesan. Put the eggs, salt, and pepper. Bake for 15 to 20 minutes.
3. Cook the onion for 5 minutes, then the garlic. Put the tomato paste. Add the ground beef, put salt and pepper. Cook, then put aside.
4. Cook marinara sauce; put pepper, red pepper flakes, and ground pepper. Stir.
5. Take out the noodles and cut them in half widthwise, and then cut them again into 3 pieces. Put 2 noodles at the bottom of the dish, then layer the parmesan and mozzarella shreds alternately.
6. Bake for 30 minutes. Garnish and serve.

Nutrition:
Calories: 508, Fat: 39 g, Protein: 33 g, Carbs: 8 g

111. Creamy Tuscan Garlic Chicken

Preparation Time: 15 minutes
Cooking Time: 30 minutes
Servings: 4
Ingredients:

- 1 lb. chicken breast
- ½ cup chicken broth
- ½ cup parmesan cheese
- ½ cup sun-dried tomatoes
- 1 cup heavy cream
- 1 cup spinach
- 2 Tbsp. olive oil
- 1 tsp. garlic powder
- 1 tsp. Italian seasoning

Directions:

1. Cook the chicken using olive oil at medium heat for 5 minutes, put aside.
2. Combine the heavy cream, garlic powder, Italian seasoning, parmesan cheese, and chicken broth. Add the sundried tomatoes and spinach and simmer. Add the chicken back and serve.

Nutrition:
Calories: 368, Fat: 0 g, Protein: 30 g, Carbs: 7 g

112. Ancho Macho Chili

Preparation Time: 20 minutes
Cooking Time: 1 hour and 30 minutes
Servings: 4
Ingredients:
- 2 lb. lean sirloin
- 1 tsp. salt
- 0.25 tsp. pepper
- 1 Tbsp. olive oil
- Onion
- Chili Powder
- 7 oz. can tomato with green chilis
- ½ cup chicken broth
- 2 cloves garlic

Directions:
1. Heat the oven to a temperature of 350°F. Coat beef with pepper and salt.
2. Cook a third of the beef. Cook the onion for a few minutes. Put in the last four ingredients and simmer. Add in the beef with all its juices, and cook for 2 hours. Stir and serve.

Nutrition:
Calories: 644, Fat: 40 g, Protein: 58 g, Net Carbs: 6 g

113. Chicken Supreme Pizza

Preparation Time: 25 minutes
Cooking Time: 30 minutes
Servings: 4-8
Ingredients:
- 5 oz. cooked chicken breast
- 1.5 cups almond flour
- 1 tsp. Baking Powder
- Salt half-tsp.
- 0.25 cup water
- 1 Red Onion
- 1 Red Pepper
- 1 Green Pepper
- 1 cup Mozzarella Cheese

Directions:
1. Heat-up the oven to a temperature of 400°F.
2. Blend the flour with both the salt and baking powder. Put the water and the oil into the flour mixture to make the dough. Flatten the dough. Dump out the dough. Press it out, and coat the pan with oil.
3. Bake within 12 minutes. Remove, then sprinkle with cheese, and then add chicken, pepper, and onion. Bake again for 15 minutes, slice, and serve.

Nutrition:
Calories: 310, Fat: 12 g, Protein: 16 g, Net Carbs: 4 g, Fiber: 10 g,

114. **Baked Jerked Chicken**

Preparation Time: 20 minutes
Cooking Time: 1 hour and 30 minutes
Servings: 4
Ingredients:
- 2 lb. chicken thighs
- 2 tsps. Olive Oil
- 2 tsps. Apple Cider Vinegar
- 1 tsp. salt
- 1 tsp. powdered onion
- ½ tsp. garlic
- ½ tsp. nutmeg
- ½ tsp. pepper
- ½ tsp. powdered ginger
- ½ tsp. powdered cayenne
- 0.25 tsp. cinnamon
- 0.25 tsp. dried thyme

Directions:
1. Mix all the ingredients, excluding the chicken. Stir in the prepared chicken pieces. Stir well.
2. Marinade for 4 hours. Heat the oven to a temperature of 375°F.
3. Cook for 1.25 hours. Adjust to broil chicken for 4 minutes. Serve.

Nutrition:
Calories: 185, Fat: 12 g Protein: 16 g, Net Carbs: 4 g Fiber: 0 g

115. Chicken Schnitzel

Preparation Time: 15 minutes
Cooking Time: 15 minutes
Servings: 3
Ingredients:
- 1 lb. chicken breast
- 0.5 cups almond flour
- 1 egg
- ½ Tbsp. powdered garlic
- ½ Tbsp. powdered onion
- Keto-Safe Oil

Directions:
1. Combine the garlic powder, flour, and onion in a bowl. Separately, beat the egg.
2. With a mallet, lb. out the chicken. Put the chicken in the egg mixture. Then roll well through the flour.
3. Take a deep-frying pan and Heat the oil to medium-high temperature.
4. Add chicken in batches. Fry. Pat dry and serve.

Nutrition:
Calories: 541, Fat: 17 g, Protein: 61 g, Net carbs: 32 g, Fiber: 0 g

116. Broccoli and Chicken Casserole

Preparation Time: 15 minutes
Cooking Time: 10 minutes
Servings: 4
Ingredients:
- 1 ½ lb. chicken breast
- 8 oz. softened cream cheese
- 0.5 cups heavy cream
- 1 tsp. powdered garlic
- 1 tsp. powdered onion
- ½ tsp. salt
- ½ tsp. pepper
- 2 cups broccoli florets
- 1 cup mozzarella
- 1 cup parmesan

Directions:
1. Heat the oven to a temperature of 400°F.
2. Combine the cream cheese with pepper and salt. Stir in the cubed chicken.
3. Put in the baking dish. Put the broccoli into the chicken-cheese mixture.
4. Top the dish with cheese, bake for about 26 minutes and remove. Take off the foil and bake again for 10 minutes. Serve.

Nutrition:
Calories: 391, Fat: 25 g, Protein: 21 g, Net carbs: 20 g, Fiber: 0g

117. Baked Fish with Lemon Butter

Preparation Time: 15 minutes
Cooking Time: 15 minutes
Servings: 2
Ingredients:
- 12 oz white fish fillets
- 1 Tbsp. olive oil
- Pepper
- Salt
- 1 medium-sized broccoli
- 2 Tbsp. butter
- 1 tsp. garlic paste
- 1 medium-sized lemon

Directions:
1. Heat the oven to a temperature of 430°F.
2. Set the fish out onto a parchment paper, and put pepper and salt. Pour over olive oil and lemon slices. Bake for 15 minutes.
3. Steam the broccoli for 5 minutes. Put aside.
4. Heat the butter, then stir in zest, garlic, remaining lemon slices, and broccoli. Cook for 2 minutes before serving.

Nutrition:
Calories: 276, Fat: 15 g, Protein: 34 g, Net Carbs: 1 g, Fiber: 0 g

CHAPTER 12:

28-DAY MEAL PLAN

Grocery List

Now that you know the benefits of keto for adults above the age of 50, you are ready to jump on the bandwagon. Here is the ultimate keto food list for a successful diet:

- Seafood: We love wild salmon, mussels, tuna, shrimps, crab.
- Low-carb Vegetables: We recommend stocking up on spinach, zucchini, kale, broccoli, cabbage.
- Low sugar Fruits: You can buy anything from berries, lemon, coconut, avocados, and tomatoes.
- Meat and Poultry: Get yourself chicken, venison, lamb, beef, or even turkey. Red meat can also be consumed but in minimal quantities.
- Eggs
- Nuts and Seeds: Buy some flaxseeds, chia seeds, pecans, walnuts, almonds, hazelnuts, etc.
- Dairy: Cheese, plain Greek yogurt, cream, and butter should be on everyone's keto list!
- Oils: Because it can get boring, buy varying oils for your kitchen cabinet, including olive oil, coconut oil, coconut butter, avocado oil, and nut oils.
- Condiments: Condiments such as olive oil mayonnaise, oil-based salad dressings, unsweetened ketchup, and mustard are keto-approved condiments.
- Dark Chocolate: The best way to enjoy chocolate guilt-free.

A Ketogenic diet has been proven to be beneficial for people of all ages, but it has also been gaining popularity amongst people above the age of fifty. The benefits of a keto diet are significant and should be preferred over a high carbohydrate diet that is commonly known to be good for older people.

Meal Plan

Day	Breakfast	Lunch	Dinner
1	Chocolate Protein Pancakes	Meatballs	Beef Stew
2	Frittata	Rainbow Mason Jar Salad	Coconut Shrimp
3	Bacon and Zucchini Muffins	Fish Cakes	Sausage Stuffed Zucchini Boats
4	Blueberry Pancake Bites	Lasagna Stuffed Peppers	Balsamic Steaks
5	Pretzels	Korean Ground Beef Bowl	Chicken Pan with Veggies and Pesto
6	Breakfast Omelet with Mushrooms	Shrimp Lettuce Wraps with Buffalo Sauce	Cabbage Soup with Beef
7	Morning Coconut Porridge	Poke Bowl with Salmon and Veggies	Cauliflower Rice Soup with Chicken
8	Sesame Keto Bagels	Thai Cucumber Noodle Salad	Quick Pumpkin Soup
9	Baked Eggs in Avocado Halves	Wrapped Bacon Cheeseburger	Fresh Avocado Soup
10	Spicy Cream Cheese Pancakes	Hearty Lunch Salad with Broccoli and Bacon	Beef Stew
11	Frittata	Rainbow Mason Jar Salad	Coconut Shrimp
12	Bacon and Zucchini Muffins	Fish Cakes	Sausage Stuffed Zucchini Boats
13	Blueberry Pancake Bites	Lasagna Stuffed Peppers	Balsamic Steaks
14	Pretzels	Korean Ground Beef Bowl	Chicken Pan with Veggies and Pesto

15	Breakfast Omelet with Mushrooms	Shrimp Lettuce Wraps with Buffalo Sauce	Cabbage Soup with Beef
16	Breakfast Omelet with Mushrooms	Shrimp Lettuce Wraps with Buffalo Sauce	Cabbage Soup with Beef
17	Morning Coconut Porridge	Poke Bowl with Salmon and Veggies	Cauliflower Rice Soup with Chicken
18	Sesame Keto Bagels	Thai Cucumber Noodle Salad	Quick Pumpkin Soup
19	Baked Eggs in Avocado Halves	Wrapped Bacon Cheeseburger	Fresh Avocado Soup
20	Spicy Cream Cheese Pancakes	Hearty Lunch Salad with Broccoli and Bacon	Beef Stew
21	Chocolate Protein Pancakes	Meatballs	Beef Stew
22	Frittata	Rainbow Mason Jar Salad	Coconut Shrimp
23	Bacon and Zucchini Muffins	Fish Cakes	Sausage Stuffed Zucchini Boats
24	Blueberry Pancake Bites	Lasagna Stuffed Peppers	Balsamic Steaks
25	Pretzels	Korean Ground Beef Bowl	Chicken Pan with Veggies and Pesto
26	Breakfast Omelet with Mushrooms	Shrimp Lettuce Wraps with Buffalo Sauce	Cabbage Soup with Beef
27	Chocolate Protein Pancakes	Poke Bowl with Salmon and Veggies	Cauliflower Rice Soup with Chicken
28	Frittata	Thai Cucumber Noodle Salad	Quick Pumpkin Soup

CONCLUSION

The Keto diet is at rage right now. For many people, selling books about keto is just one of many indicators of a booming trend. While any diet can work for anyone, keto diets are trendy among women over 50. It's no wonder—it's easy to get started. Every woman wants to look young for the rest of her life. With the growing age, it is tough to maintain youthfulness. When you become over 50, your body stops producing certain hormones, which causes menopause and both mental and physical strain.

Your metabolism slows down, and you become less enthusiastic about taking up new things in life. You gain weight with every passing year, and this makes you look dull. It is also the time when you will bombard with many problems causing you to be depressed. The only way to maintain youthfulness is by reducing the amount of weight you carry on your body. The Keto Diet plan does just that. It helps you keep a good figure and gives you the energy to do things in life.

Keto meals for women are entirely different because when we come to this diet, we must be very cautious about what we put in our stomachs. The meals during Keto Diet are altogether different as compared to the normal ones. The keto diet for women needs to be followed strictly to get the best result.

Stop eating carbs—in other words, cut out all sugar and flour. It includes fruit and vegetables as well. Eat proteins (preferably clean sources) for every meal instead. Animal-based foods include eggs, meat, poultry, fish, cheese, and cottage cheese. Vegetable-based foods include cheese (non-fat), coconut oil, olive oil, avocado oil, and avocados (in moderation) should be eaten sparingly. Ketogenic diets are known for being extremely useful for weight loss. Many studies have shown that it helps in losing 10-15% excess weight within a month of following the keto diet. But, women over 50 are usually observed to gain weight on a Ketogenic diet.

Avoid all fruits (other than berries), except green vegetables such as green beans, broccoli, and leafy greens. Water can substitute for soda/juice/sugar/sweetened drinks with no adverse effects on benefits. Peanut or almond butter is okay, and seeds such as flax and chia are good too if they are unsweetened.

Choose fat-based dishes over carbs whenever possible. Choose fish or chicken over red meat.

Printed in Great Britain
by Amazon